D0635477

PHILIP ALLAN

LITERATURE GUIDE

FOR GCSE

LORD OF THE FLIES
WILLIAM GOLDING

Robert Francis
and Martin Walker

 **PHILIP ALLAN**

With thanks to Jeanette Weatherall for reviewing the manuscript of this book

Philip Allan, an imprint of Hodder Education, an Hachette UK company, Market Place, Deddington, Oxfordshire OX15 0SE

Orders

Bookpoint Ltd, 130 Milton Park, Abingdon, Oxfordshire OX14 4SB
tel: 01235 827827
fax: 01235 400401
e-mail: education@bookpoint.co.uk
Lines are open 9.00 a.m.–5.00 p.m., Monday to Saturday, with a 24-hour message answering service. You can also order through the Philip Allan Updates website: www.philipallan.co.uk

© Philip Allan Publishers 2010
ISBN 978-1-4441-1021-0
First printed 2010

Impression number 5 4 3
Year 2015 2014 2013

All rights reserved; no part of this publication may be reproduced, stored in a retrieval system, or transmitted, in any other form or by any means, electronic, mechanical, photocopying, recording or otherwise without either the prior written permission of Philip Allan Updates or a licence permitting restricted copying in the United Kingdom issued by the Copyright Licensing Agency Ltd, Saffron House, 6–10 Kirby Street, London EC1N 8TS.

Printed in Spain

Hachette UK's policy is to use papers that are natural, renewable and recyclable products and made from wood grown in sustainable forests. The logging and manufacturing processes are expected to conform to the environmental regulations of the country of origin.

Contents

Getting the most from this book and website

How to use this guide

You may find it useful to read sections of this guide when you need them, rather than reading it from start to finish. For example, you could decide to read the *Plot and structure* section in conjunction with the novel or the *Context* section before you start reading the novel. The sections relating to assessments will be especially useful in the weeks leading up to the exam.

The following features have been used throughout this guide:

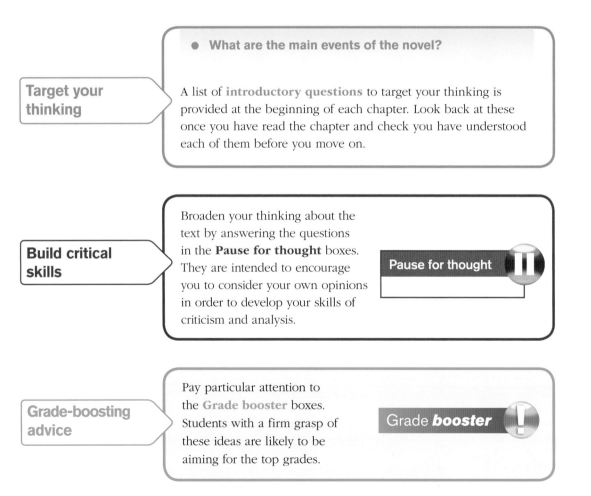

● **What are the main events of the novel?**

Target your thinking

A list of **introductory questions** to target your thinking is provided at the beginning of each chapter. Look back at these once you have read the chapter and check you have understood each of them before you move on.

Build critical skills

Broaden your thinking about the text by answering the questions in the **Pause for thought** boxes. They are intended to encourage you to consider your own opinions in order to develop your skills of criticism and analysis.

Pause for thought

Grade-boosting advice

Pay particular attention to the **Grade booster** boxes. Students with a firm grasp of these ideas are likely to be aiming for the top grades.

Grade *booster*

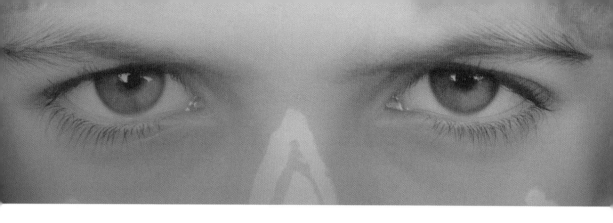

Key quotations are highlighted for you, and you may wish to use these as evidence in your examination answers.

Key quotation

'The rules!...You're breaking the rules'
(p. 99)

Be exam-ready

The **Grade focus** sections explain how you may be assessed and distinguish between higher and foundation responses.

Grade *focus*

Get the top grades

Use the **Text focus** boxes to practise evaluating the text in detail and looking for evidence to support your understanding.

Text **focus**

Develop evaluation skills

Review your learning

Use the **Review your learning** sections to test your knowledge after you have read each chapter. Answers to the questions are provided in the final section of the guide.

Test your knowledge

Don't forget to go online for even more free revision activities and self-tests:
www.philipallan.co.uk/literatureguidesonline

Introduction

How to approach the text

A novel is, above all, a narrative. A large part of the storyteller's art is to make you want to find out what happens next and, therefore, to keep you reading on to the end. In order to study *Lord of the Flies* and enjoy it, you need to keep a close track of the events that take place in it. This guide will help you to do that but you may also benefit from keeping your own notes on the main events and who is involved in them.

However, any novel consists of much more than its events. You need to know the story well to do well in your exam, but if you spend too much time simply retelling the story, you will not get a high mark. You also need to keep track of a number of other features.

Take notice of the setting of the novel (where the events take place) and how this influences the story. Get to know the characters too and understand how Golding lets us know what they are like. Notice what they say and do, and what other people say about them. Think about why they behave in the way they do: what their motives are, and what clues the author gives us about them.

As you read on, you will notice themes (the ideas explored by the author in the book). You may find it easier to think about these while not actually reading the book, especially if you discuss them with other people. You should also try to think about the style of the novel, especially on a second reading. 'Style' means how the author tells the story.

All these aspects of the novel are dealt with in this guide but you should always try to notice them for yourself. The guide is no substitute for a careful and thoughtful reading of the text.

Other interpretations

There have been several film versions of *Lord of the Flies*. While it is good to watch one or more of these, it is important for you to write about the novel and how it is written and not about the film version.

In 1963 the renowned director Peter Brook produced a black-and-white version of *Lord of the Flies* that is true to the original novel. In 1990 Harry Hook reinvented the novel in his Americanised colour film. This is less true to the original story but follows the main ideas and characters fairly closely.

Page references

Page references are given for the Faber and Faber 2002 edition of the text (ISBN 978-0-571-19147-5).

Context

- What does the term 'context' mean?
- What does the context of the novel tell the reader about its purpose?
- How does Golding relate the events on the island to those in the wider world?
- What use does he make of the fears of people in the 1950s?
- How has Golding used his own experiences in the novel?

It is useful to know about the context of the text, as it explains many of the author's ideas, but if you are studying the AQA, OCR and CCEA specifications, you will not be assessed on context in the examination. Context is assessed by WJEC only.

The context of a novel means the circumstances at the time it was written — the social, historical and literary factors that influenced what the author wrote. *Lord of the Flies* was written in the early 1950s and published in 1954. The world in which it was written is different from the one in which we live today. In order to understand the book you need some knowledge of the context in which it was created. In addition, you should show a grasp of the context and setting when writing about the book as part of an English literature course.

This is not meant to be a history lesson, but some understanding of the time at which it was written will give you a deeper insight into the book. Here are some points to consider:

- The people of Britain had just been through the Second World War.
- Food was still being rationed in Britain.
- It was thought that there might be a nuclear war between Western countries and the Soviet Union.
- Golding worked as a teacher in a boys' school.
- Britain was having to come to terms with the loss of the British Empire.
- Public schools still produced most of Britain's leaders and top professionals.
- Nazi Germany had adopted a system of rewarding the strong and attacking the weak.

Grade *booster*

To achieve a grade A* you have to identify and comment on the impact of social, cultural and historical contexts.

William Golding later in life in 1983

TopFoto

- The adults the boys wish could help them are the same ones who are fighting the war that has led to the boys being stranded.
- The boys are rescued by a naval officer who is part of the war, yet he asks if they have been 'Having a war or something' (p. 223).

The Second World War

Britain declared war on Germany on 3 September 1939 and the war in Europe lasted for almost six years. In the novel Golding explores some of the ideas that lay behind the Nazi government of Germany.

- The German leader Adolf Hitler adapted ideas from science and philosophy for his own ends. Compare Hitler's ideas of racial purity and the supremacy of the Aryan race with Darwin's theory of natural selection and survival of the fittest (see the *Themes* section of this guide for more detail). On the island, the boys have varying degrees of physical and mental strength. You need to think about which characteristics Golding portrays as gaining supremacy.
- One of the most feared of the Nazi organisations was the SS (*Schutzstaffel*: defence corps). The SS was fiercely loyal to Hitler and was renowned for never showing human weakness. The often brutal way in which the SS treated its enemies is similar to the way Jack uses Roger to terrify the other boys into submission.

The Hitler Youth in Nazi Germany

TopFoto

● Millions of ordinary Germans were involved in the war and some carried out terrible atrocities without question. You can find parallels for this in the novel.

Golding's war experience

During the Second World War, Golding served in the British Navy, on several different ships, and was in charge of specially adapted landing craft for the D-day landings in Normandy, so he witnessed at first hand the horrors of war. He came to the conclusion that human beings are not naturally kind and that even children are capable of incredible cruelty if the circumstances demand or even simply allow it.

Golding was interested in the way that violence can develop from innocent beginnings. Here is an extract from one of his autobiographical works, *Scenes from a Life,* in which he discusses such a childhood accident:

> I swung the bat in a semicircle, missed the ball but hit José with the wooden bat across the side of the head. Instantly he turned and ran for home, one hand holding the side of his head. I was the one who made a noise, anguished to think of the awful thing I had done. But he made not a sound. He always was the silent one. I trundled after him, whimpering and wondering what I should tell mam and dad, or what he would.
>
> I trundled back across the Common and down the road to the Green, my fears growing deeper. I can just remember them. I ended at the house, terrified and now as silent as my brother. I remember no more. But years later my parents told me that José had described the whole scene to them. He wasn't really hurt they said. But I crept in to the house with my terror and hid from everyone else under the dining room table.

The violence in *Lord of the Flies* starts as a game. The game goes too far and the potential for the extreme savagery that follows can be seen in all the boys except Piggy and perhaps Simon.

You can probably think of examples from your own childhood of situations that got out of hand. A typical 'play fight' can easily end up becoming more serious, and young children don't always see the boundaries between play and reality. For many of the younger boys in the novel, this is exactly what happens: children's games get out of hand.

The Cold War

Following the Second World War, Britain's former ally, the Soviet Union, became the potential enemy of the West. The major nuclear powers were the USA and the Soviet Union, with the USA's NATO (North Atlantic Treaty Organization) allies such as Britain and France following closely behind. Throughout the 1950s, people in Britain feared the threat of Soviet nuclear

attack. The Allied nuclear attacks on Nagasaki and Hiroshima at the end of the Second World War brought home to people what nuclear war meant. The Soviet and NATO forces were separated by the flimsiest of borders, and nuclear weapons situated in Ukraine could have reached the UK in such a short time that few people would have survived even if British missiles had been fired as soon as the attack was detected. The nuclear stand-off became known as Mutually Assured Destruction (MAD), as it would have led to the destruction of both attacker and attacked — no one could win.

The novel is obviously set against the backdrop of a nuclear war. However, it also subtly explores the idea of Mutually Assured Destruction within its own plot. The final fire destroys the world of the island. If the naval officer had not arrived, how would Jack's tribe have survived its 'victory'?

At the time the novel was written nuclear war was a real threat

Life in 1950s Britain

Rationing

Food rationing had been a part of people's lives in Britain since the start of the Second World War. School children in the early 1950s had grown up without knowing what it was like to have a wide range of food readily available.

The lack of food in Britain throughout the war and even into the early post-war years was a major influence on people's lives. Although people had enough food to survive, meat in any quantity and imported fruit such as oranges and bananas became luxuries. Food plays a major part in *Lord of the Flies* — look at the availability of food on the island. It is the desire to hunt for meat that causes many of the problems between the boys. When they first land on the island, they collect food whenever they are hungry. Later, hunting becomes a major driving force behind Jack's actions, although this is about far deeper urges than just hunger for food.

Hardship

Large areas of British cities had suffered severe damage from German bombing. By the 1950s, rebuilding work was under way but there were still many devastated areas. There was a shortage of many everyday items and 'making do and mending' was still common practice in most homes. Clothes were difficult to obtain and so repairing them was essential. We

> ### Key quotation
>
> **He tried to convey the compulsion to track down and kill that was swallowing him up.**
>
> (p. 51)

may see hardships in today's society, but for very different reasons and of a very different kind.

Keeping up appearances was a very British way of dealing with hardship. Look at the importance that clothes play in representing civilised society in the novel. When Ralph, Piggy, Sam and Eric go to Castle Rock at the end of the book they attempt to dress themselves as English schoolboys, as though this will make their requests more acceptable to Jack.

Attitudes

The Second World War cost Britain its empire. At its height, the British Empire was the greatest the world had known. It spread across the whole globe and the saying 'The sun never sets on the British Empire' had been literally true: somewhere in the empire it was daytime no matter what the time was in Britain. In Britain, the upper and middle classes had grown up with the idea that it was natural for them to be in charge and to organise others. This idea is expressed several times in the novel: that simply being English means that certain things are expected. See the section on *The Coral Island* for further examples of typical British grit.

Knowing your place was still an accepted idea in Britain. It was difficult for people born into poor, working-class backgrounds to rise in society. At the start of the novel, the boys have a clear sense of their own relative importance.

> ### *Text* focus
>
> Look at the passage in Chapter 1 from 'I could swim when I was five. Daddy taught me.' to 'About the atom bomb? They're all dead' (pp. 8–9).
>
> What does what Piggy and Ralph say show us about the importance of grown-ups to them?
>
> What negative impact have grown-ups had on their lives?

Class

In the 1950s the class system in Britain was still rigid. It is still in place today but has changed in some ways over the last 50 years.

The upper class

The upper class consisted mainly of aristocratic families with inherited money that came mostly from huge estates of land. It is worth reflecting that in the early part of the twentieth century, 1% of the population owned 99% of the wealth. The aristocracy had been in decline since the late 1930s but still held great power. The wealthiest man in Britain is still the Duke of Westminster, the country's largest landowner. Upper-class boys were educated at prestigious public schools such as Eton, Harrow and Marlborough (see the section on schools on p. 10).

The middle class

This was a much wider group than the upper class. The middle classes made their money through business or the professions. Such people would want their children to have a good start in life, and would often imitate the upper-class practice of sending their children, particularly boys, to public schools — probably 'minor' public schools that did not have the status of Eton or Harrow.

The boys in *Lord of the Flies* are typical examples of middle-class children of the 1950s. There is no evidence that their families are particularly wealthy: Ralph's father is in the Navy and Piggy's aunt does not seem to be wealthy.

The working class

As the name says, working-class people worked for a living. Many worked in the factories, shops and businesses owned by the middle classes. Working-class education had usually been poor in Britain. Until the Butler Education Act of 1944, many children left school at the age of 14 with only a basic schooling.

Before the Second World War it had been virtually impossible for working-class people to mix on equal terms with their 'betters'. In the 1950s the situation gradually began to change, with new opportunities in the Britain that was emerging from the wreckage of the war. This has continued to develop up to the present day.

1950s schoolboys

Public schools and grammar schools

The class system and the education system were closely linked. Public schools were, and still are, fee-paying schools. By contrast the 1944 Education Act introduced free grammar schools across the country. These were often single-sex schools and required pupils to pass an exam at the age of 11 — the 11-plus. Grammar schools kept the uniform and traditions of the public schools and were seen as providing an academic education for bright children who could otherwise not afford it. Children who failed the 11-plus went to secondary modern schools to learn more practical subjects. In practice, many more middle-class than working-class children went to grammar schools, while most working-class children went to the secondary moderns.

The boys in *Lord of the Flies* appear to be typical of the kinds of boys who would go to public schools at age 13 or grammar schools at 11. Their behaviour and dialogue are masterfully portrayed by Golding.

When you discuss this aspect of the novel, you should remember that Golding was a qualified teacher who worked at a boys' grammar school for many years, both before and after the war.

> **Key quotation**
>
> 'We'll have to have "Hands up" like at school.'
>
> (p. 31)

> **Pause for thought**
>
> How has education changed since the 1950s? Think about:
> - how teaching has changed
> - how the behaviour of children has changed
> - how the class system has changed — is this still connected to education in the same way?

Boys' adventure books

Lord of the Flies follows a tradition of adventure books aimed mainly at boys — girls were not encouraged to seek adventure before the 1950s. In Chapter 2 the boys liken their situation to *Treasure Island, Swallows and Amazons* and *The Coral Island*. Such books were very popular, particularly with young boys such as those in the novel.

Golding's interest in the existence of evil

The novel reflects in several ways Golding's interest in the existence of evil, including the idea of the beast, the boys' degeneration into savagery and the background of the war. The title of the book is meant to be a reference to the Devil or Beelzebub (the Hebrew word for the Devil), which is the God of the Fly (translated as Lord of the Flies), which is most clearly evident when the pig's head appears to speak to Simon.

A modern reader's interpretation

Since the novel was written, society has changed and our view of the novel will be very different from that of readers when it was originally published in 1954.

> **Text focus**
>
> Look at the end of Chapter 8 from '"You are a silly little boy," said the Lord of the Flies...' (pp. 157–59).
>
> What does the Lord of the Flies say in this section about evil?
>
> Why is it significant that it is Simon and no one else who hears/imagines this?
>
> The notion that there is evil in all of us is explored throughout the novel. Pick out three other sections of the novel where the theme of evil is explored. Make notes on what happens, pick out some relevant and useful quotations and explore what Golding is trying to say in the novel about evil.

Pause for thought

Using all the material from this section, draw up a chart of what life was like in the 1950s and compare that to life today.

Life in 1950s	Life today	Differences
Still a big division in class, with lower, middle and upper class clearly defined	Class differences not so clearly defined	While there is still a class system today, it is less clearly defined than it was in the 1950s

Grade *focus*

Only in the WJEC exam is context assessed directly.

The exam consists of three questions on *Lord of the Flies* of which you have to answer two. Question A is a compulsory passage from the text that does not assess AO4, but does assess AO1 and AO2.

You then have to answer one of questions B and C, which assess AO4 as well as AO1.

You will be asked a question on the text and will be expected to show awareness of context in your answer.

For example:

What do you think of Jack and the way he is presented in the novel?

To achieve a C grade you would normally be expected to write about the context of the book, make some comments on your own views and how the novel relates to your own experiences. You might say something about how the book has influenced other people and what they have written since it was published.

For an A* you will need to be clear when you write about the social/cultural and historical context of the book and write clearly about the time the novel was written and set and how this has influenced others by writing either in a similar style or about similar themes. Your answer will be more exploratory than for a C grade and your ideas will be more detailed and original.

Review your learning

(Answers are given on p. 91.)

1. What is meant by the context of a novel?

2. What do the events on a paradise island show us about human behaviour in the wider world?

3. How do 1950s' fears of atomic war influence your reading of the novel?

4. How are order and class represented in the novel?

More interactive questions and answers online.

Plot and structure

- **What are the main events of the novel?**
- **How do the main storylines develop through the novel?**
- **What indications are there about the passage of time in the novel?**

Chapter 1 The sound of the shell

- Ralph and Piggy call the other boys together.
- Ralph is made leader but Jack keeps the choir.
- Ralph, Jack and Simon learn that they are on an island.

The novel opens with Ralph clambering through the jungle towards the lagoon. He is accompanied by Piggy (who has not yet told Ralph his nickname).

From the boys' conversation we learn that they were in a plane that had been attacked and which then crashed on the island. It soon dawns on the boys that there are probably no adults left alive.

Grade *booster*

The reference to the coral island is a link to the novel *The Coral Island* by R. M. Ballantyne (see notes on boys' adventure books in the *Context* section.). The boys in Ballantyne's novel behave impeccably and are models of old-fashioned Britishness. This novel was clearly in Golding's mind when writing *Lord of the Flies*. Commenting on this, in relation to the question, will help you gain higher marks in the examination.

Pause for thought

…the creature was a party of boys…   (p. 15)

The choir and Jack are compared to a creature, which makes them seem less human. Why is this appropriate?

The plane crash is a deliberate ploy by Golding: the boys have no means of reconstructing England from the wreckage. They are alone with whatever tools and other aids to survival they can fashion for themselves.

Piggy tells Ralph that he heard the pilot saying that an atom bomb had gone off and no one was left to look for them. He finds a conch shell and, when Ralph blows the conch, boys begin to appear from the jungle. The younger boys wait patiently to be told what to do.

As soon as Jack arrives, leading his choir, he begins to assert himself, and he is the only boy who speaks to Ralph on equal terms.

Text focus

Read the passage from 'The children who came along the beach' to 'eccentric clothing' (pp. 14–15).

Notice that Golding uses an interesting **foreshadowing** technique here. Twice he presents an animal image to describe what the boys seem to see, before revealing to us what is really there:

> Here, the eye was first attracted to a black, bat-like creature that danced on the sand, and only later perceived the body above it. The bat was the child's shadow...

> Within the diamond haze of the beach something dark was fumbling along. Ralph saw it first, and watched till the intentness of his gaze drew all eyes that way. Then the creature stepped from mirage on to clear sand, and they saw that the darkness was not all shadow but mostly clothing. The creature was a party of boys...

Both metaphors suggest that the heat of the island plays tricks on the boys and makes them imagine things that are not really there. Golding makes us see things from the boys' point of view. We too are tricked at first, before discovering the reality. It is significant that both 'creatures' are dark and vaguely threatening, despite the brilliant sunshine.

How successful do you think this foreshadowing technique is?

The conch: a symbol of power

Alamy/Steve Taylor ARPS

Ralph lifts the conch and says that there should be a chief to decide things. Jack immediately says that he should be the chief. The boys, however, attracted by Ralph's quiet authority and the fact that he has blown the conch, quickly elect him as chief.

Key quotation

But there was a stillness about Ralph as he sat that marked him out...

(p. 19)

Ralph, Jack and Simon explore the area and find a piglet trapped in the undergrowth: Jack draws his knife, but hesitates, which allows the animal to escape. This is the reader's first glimpse of Jack's willingness to kill. Though he hesitates here, this incident is a clear indication that he is capable of being savage.

Key quotation

...he hadn't: because of the enormity of the knife descending and cutting into living flesh; because of the unbearable blood. (p. 29)

Chapter 2 Fire on the mountain

- The small boys begin to worry about a beast.
- A signal fire is lit, with the choir responsible for keeping it going.
- The forest catches fire and at least one boy is killed.

Jack interrupts the second meeting to announce that they will need hunters to catch pigs. He gets excited by the idea of inventing rules, especially so that those who break them can be punished.

Ralph decides that the conch will be passed to anyone who asks to speak and that the person with the conch will not be interrupted. The use of the conch is a child's version of order.

One of the smaller boys says that he has seen a giant snake that he calls the 'beastie', which came at night and tried to eat him.

Ralph tells the boys that they need to light a fire on the mountain top to attract the attention of passing ships. Jack realises that Piggy's glasses can be used to light the fire.

Jack begins to change the rules even at this early stage, mostly to suit himself, foreshadowing the way he behaves later in the novel.

Ralph announces that the conch counts no matter where it is used.

Piggy notices that the fire has set the surrounding forest ablaze and at least one of the younger boys might have been caught in the forest fire.

> **Key quotation**
>
> 'We ought to have more rules. Where the conch is, that's a meeting.'
>
> (p. 42)

> **Key quotation**
>
> 'That little 'un—' gasped Piggy – 'him with the mark on his face, I don't see him. Where is he now?'
>
> (p. 46)

> **Grade *booster***
>
> Exploring the symbolism of fire can help you achieve a higher grade. The fire is a symbol of the power of the forces of nature. The boys think they can control the situation, but stopping the fire is soon beyond their power.

> **Pause for thought**
>
> Many of the most important symbols of the novel are introduced in this chapter: the fire, the conch, Piggy's glasses and the beast. What do we learn about each of these symbols in this chapter?

Chapter 3 Huts on the beach

- Jack becomes more interested in hunting.
- Ralph tries to get the boys to build shelters.

> **Pause for thought**
>
> The boys begin to feel an impact, and even a threat, from the natural world that surrounds them. They are unsure how to react. The small boys are scared and even Jack feels he is being hunted. How would you explain their fears at this point? Are they simply 'imagining things', or is there something real to be afraid of?

Jack is in the forest on his own, tracking pigs. He has now made himself a spear and still carries a large knife.

Ralph realises that Jack is intent on killing but asks for his help with the shelters. Jack insists that he needs to catch meat for the group. Ralph and Jack both come close to losing their tempers but refuse to compromise their own point of view.

The 'littluns' are becoming frightened at night because they think that there is something in the forest that will come to get them. Jack feels that he is not alone when he is in the forest but that he is being hunted even though he is supposedly the one hunting.

> **Key quotation**
>
> **They walked along, two continents of experience and feeling, unable to communicate.**
>
> (p. 56)

Chapter 4 Painted faces and long hair

- Smoke from a ship is seen on the horizon.
- The fire has gone out.
- Jack nearly stands up to Ralph.
- Piggy's glasses are partly broken by Jack.
- The boys have a feast of roast pig.

The boys play on the beach and we are introduced to some of the other characters, such as Henry, Percival, Roger and Maurice. Jack is experimenting with camouflaging his face so that the pigs cannot see him so easily. However, as we will gradually see, this face painting is also a means of escaping from the constraints of civilised society.

Jack with a painted face

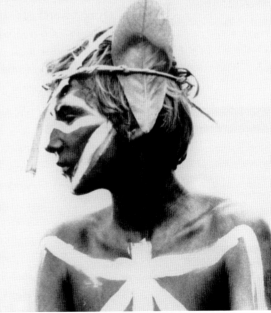

> **Key quotation**
>
> **...the mask was a thing on its own, behind which Jack hid, liberated from shame and self-consciousness.**
>
> (p. 66)

> **Text focus**
>
> Read the passage beginning 'Jack was standing under a tree' and ending with 'The mask compelled them' (pp. 65–67).
>
> What do you think makes Jack want to paint his face and what effect does this have on his behaviour? (Think about connections to ancient societies that also practised this ceremonial behaviour.)

Alamy/Photos 12

Ralph sees smoke on the horizon and realises there is a ship passing by. Ralph races up the mountain and finds that the fire is dead and that the members of the choir who were supposed to be looking after it have left.

Jack appears with the hunters. They are carrying a dead pig slung on a stick.

Key quotation

…Jack smacked Piggy's head. Piggy's glasses flew off and tinkled on the rocks. Piggy cried out in terror…

(p. 75)

There is another confrontation between Ralph and Jack but Piggy speaks up and allows Jack to attack him instead of Ralph. One eye of Piggy's glasses is broken.

Ralph asserts his authority and Jack backs down a little, but it is clear he now has the admiration of many of the boys because he has brought them meat.

The fire is relit and the boys feast on the pig.

Chapter 5 Beast from water

- Ralph calls an assembly.
- The boys find it hard to listen to sensible ideas.
- The idea of the beast is discussed.
- Jack rebels.

Ralph calls an important assembly to discuss the fire and the way the boys live on the island. At first the boys listen to his points, which are:

- No one is collecting fresh water any longer.
- The shelters have not been built properly because most of the boys got bored and gave up.
- The rocks are no longer being used as a lavatory.
- The fire is the most important thing.
- The only fire is to be on the mountain.
- There is no beast.

Grade **booster**

Higher-band answers will comment on Percival's fear of the beast from the sea, saying it is really just the fear of the unknown. This fear of the unknown, and the savagery it provokes, is a theme of the novel.

Many of the younger boys are convinced that there is a beast on the island. One of the small boys, Percival, says that the beast comes from the sea. Even Simon says that there may be a beast, which undermines Ralph in front of the others.

The rule whereby a boy must be holding the conch to speak starts to break down and Jack defies Ralph.

Jack leads the choir away and the assembly dissolves, leaving Ralph looking powerless. Ralph, Piggy and Simon are left wishing there was an adult present to tell them what to do and to reassure them.

Key quotation

'The rules…you're breaking the rules!'

'Who cares?'   (p. 99)

Grade *booster*

The remaining boys long for adult intervention. They make several ironic comments about adults:

'They wouldn't quarrel'

'Or break my specs'

'Or talk about a beast'   (p. 102)

Yet all these are aspects of many adults. Adults argue, commit acts of violence on each other and have strong superstitious beliefs. Such a comment, developed by saying that Golding is making the point that the boys are a reflection of the adult world beyond the island, is typical of higher-level candidates.

> **Key quotation**
>
> **'We're all drifting and things are going rotten. At home there was always a grown-up.'**
>
> (p. 101)

Chapter 6 Beast from air

- A dead airman parachutes on to the island.
- Sam and Eric hear something strange on the mountain.

During the night an airman lands on the island. It is ironic that the three boys get their wish of having an adult on the island, but not in the way that they expected.

Jack wants to hunt this new beast, but Ralph is less sure and admits that he is frightened.

Jack almost gets his way but Ralph asks the boys again, 'Don't you all want to be rescued?' (p. 111) and they listen to him. The older boys set off to search the only part of the island they have not yet explored, with Jack leading the way.

Simon thinks of the beast as human but cannot bring himself to tell Ralph.

Ralph takes charge again. He sets off to climb the path round the rock and finds that Jack has come too.

Jack says that the rock would make a good castle, and that it even has fresh water.

> **Key quotation**
>
> **Simon mumbled confusedly: 'I don't believe in the beast.'**
>
> (p. 114)

Chapter 7 Shadows and tall trees

- The boys nearly catch a boar.
- The hunters show they can be savage to other boys.
- There is an expedition up the mountain.
- The dead airman is seen at night, which causes panic.

Ralph notices how dirty he and the other boys have become and wishes he could look like his old self: 'Be sucking my thumb next–' (p. 120).

Grade booster

Higher-grade answers will comment on how Simon tells Ralph that he will get home safely. He does not include himself. Perhaps this is because he does not think he will get home safely and he has seen a premonition of Ralph's safe arrival home. This adds to the mystical qualities that surround Simon throughout the novel.

Grade booster

Comments such as 'It is important that the expedition to find the beast takes place at night. In daylight what was actually on the mountain might well have been obvious to the older boys. It was Jack's idea to go up at night and it is Jack who causes much of the trouble that follows' are typical of exploratory, developed and analytical responses.

Grade booster

An A* answer might explore the fact that Jack's question to the boys is a classic mistake. The boys are unlikely to challenge Ralph when he is in front of them. If Jack had simply said 'Who wants a powerful hunter like me as chief?' he might have been more successful.

This reveals that he is still attached to civilisation — in contrast with the hunters, who are becoming wilder and more like primitive savages. Simon tells Ralph that he is sure Ralph will get home safely.

The boys become excited on a hunt and form a circle around Robert. They beat him and jab him with spears, and even Ralph joins in. At one point Jack suggests that they should use a littlun in the game and actually kill him. It is not clear whether he is joking.

The boys are becoming more savage each day.

Key quotation

'Kill him! Kill him!'

All at once, Robert was screaming and struggling with the strength of frenzy. (p. 125)

Ralph asks Jack why he hates him so much.

Ralph suggests they wait until morning to go up the mountain. Jack says he is going now and challenges Ralph to join him.

Ralph leads Jack and Roger up the mountain and, just as he gets near to the body, the wind pulls the airman upright and Ralph looks straight into the rotting face of the corpse.

Chapter 8 Gift for the darkness

- The boys are told about the beast on the mountain.
- Jack leaves to set up his own tribe.
- The hunters kill a pig and leave its head on a stick.
- Jack invites the other boys to join him.
- Simon hears the Lord of the Flies.

Jack blows the conch and brings the boys together. He lies to them, saying that Ralph is a coward and that he didn't go up the mountain with them. Jack accuses Ralph of not being a proper chief.

Key quotation

'He's a coward himself.'
(p. 138)

Jack asks the boys how many of them do not want Ralph as chief. He gets no response. Jack announces that he is no longer going to be part of 'Ralph's lot' and runs away, inviting anyone who wants to hunt to join him.

Piggy suggests that the fire should be lit on the beach as it would give off smoke just the same.

A group of the younger boys has attached itself to Jack and he is still intent on hunting pigs. He now thinks that if they leave some of the pig for the beast then it will not come after them.

The hunters find a group of pigs and wound a large sow. They follow her into the forest and kill her. Jack guts the sow and cuts off the head. He places the head on a stick as a gift for the beast. When Simon finds himself in the clearing he sees the head covered in a mass of flies and thinks of it as the 'Lord of the Flies'.

Back on the beach, Ralph admits to Piggy that he is scared that they will never be rescued. Jack and the hunters arrive, stealing burning sticks and running off. Jack announces that he and his hunters are living along the beach and that they 'hunt and feast and have fun' (p. 154). He invites others to join his 'tribe'.

The hunters now have painted faces and are smeared with blood. They are turning into savages in appearance and action, and Golding refers to them as such.

Jack says there is to be a feast and anyone who wants can come. Two of the hunters end his invitation with the words 'The Chief has spoken' (p. 155). The hunters are beginning to treat Jack like a king and there are elements of worship in the way they now behave towards him.

Ralph insists that fire is the way they will be rescued but begins to sound less convincing. The boys want meat and like the idea of playing at being hunters. There appears to be an ancient instinct in them that they do not fully understand but which is beginning to take hold of them.

Simon is still watching the pig's head on a stick. He imagines that it tells him that the beast is not something that can be hunted and killed. It says that the beast is part of him.

> **Pause for thought**
>
> It is a highly significant turn of events when Jack takes his followers off to form a separate tribe. Think about how this mirrors human behaviour at all levels of life. Think of your class in school, or your local community. How far are these groups already divided into 'tribes'?

> **Key quotation**
>
> **Demoniac figures with faces of white and red and green rushed out howling...**
>
> (p. 154)

> **Key quotation**
>
> **'Fancy thinking the Beast was something you could hunt and kill!' said the head...'You knew, didn't you? I'm part of you?'**
>
> (p. 158)

Chapter 9 A view to a death

- A storm is gathering over the island.
- Simon finds the dead airman and realises what he is.
- Simon frees the airman's parachute lines.
- Jack holds a feast.
- The boys dance and chant.
- Simon is killed.
- The dead airman is blown out to sea.

Simon discovers that the beast is nothing more than a dead airman and he frees the parachute from the trees so that the body stops moving. It is important that it is Simon who finds out that the beast is simply a dead airman. Simon is seen as strange by the other boys and his rather distant nature marks him out as a victim for Jack and the hunters.

Grade *booster*

Both the airman and Simon are swept out to sea. To gain a higher mark, you could explore how this is symbolic: the beast has gone, and so has the only boy who really grasped that the beast is not a real creature but is in each of the boys. It also removes all proof of the violence. Piggy's body is also swept out to sea later on.

Ralph and Piggy visit Jack's feast and are given meat to eat. Ralph tries to assert himself as chief but Piggy warns him that there is going to be trouble. Ralph points out that there is a storm coming and that if the boys had listened to him they would now have shelters against the rain. At this, Jack leads the boys in a dance and they are soon all chanting their hunting chant. The hunters are in a circle and work themselves into a frenzy.

> ### Key quotation
>
> **...demented but partly secure society.** (p. 167)

At this point Simon appears and tries to tell the boys that the beast is simply a dead airman. They are too worked up to listen and they surround him, drive him to the beach and kill him in a savage manner.

Text focus

In Chapter 9 you should look closely at three sections:
- the opening of the chapter in which the storm is building
- the storm breaking and the climax that follows
- the eerie quiet that follows the storm

Golding uses the weather to create an atmosphere that matches the unfolding events. Notice the following phrases (p. 160):

...the build-up of clouds continued...

...the air was ready to explode.

...a brassy glare had taken the place of clear daylight.

Colours drained...

...clouds brooded.

Nothing prospered...

We sense that something bad is on its way. Golding develops this feeling as the chapter unfolds. Notice 'a sky of thunderous brass that rang with the storm-coming' and 'Evening was come, not with calm beauty but with the threat of violence' (p. 165). Piggy senses the threat and warns Ralph: 'There's going to be trouble' (p. 167).

The storm begins with a 'blink of bright light' and drops of rain. Within a few lines the 'blows of the thunder' are 'only just bearable'. The climax is heralded by a streak of lightning described as 'a blue-white scar', followed by another: 'Again the blue-white scar jagged above them' (p. 168). The scar suggests the violence that is about to explode. When it does, Golding simulates the confused frenzy of the moment from the boys' viewpoint.

The paragraphs from 'Towards midnight' (p. 169) to the end of the chapter create an entirely different atmosphere. This is the calm after the storm, and the washing out to sea of Simon's body is described in a very moving and mystical way, as if he is being taken to heaven by the 'strange, attendant creatures, with their fiery eyes and trailing vapours' (p. 170). What do you suppose Golding is describing here? Why does he not make it more obvious exactly what is happening to Simon's body?

The parachute is caught by the wind and lifts the dead parachutist over the trees and down to the beach. The boys are panicked by this and scatter into the darkness. The parachutist is blown out to sea. The sea also takes Simon's body away from the island.

Chapter 10 The shell and the glasses

- Ralph and Piggy think about Simon's death.
- Jack sets up camp on the Castle Rock.
- Jack's tribe attacks Ralph and the other boys with him.
- Piggy's glasses are stolen by Jack.

> **Key quotation**
>
> **'That was Simon.'**
>
> **'That was murder.'**
>
> (p. 172)

Ralph tries to discuss the death of Simon, which he describes as murder. Piggy tells him there was nothing they could do and that they were not really involved. Jack has set up camp on the Castle Rock. He is now acting as chief of his own tribe. Jack has had Wilfred tied up and has beaten him for some unknown crime.

Jack is now dressed and painted like a savage and gives orders without expecting to be questioned. He is behaving exactly as any all-powerful tribal leader might. He enjoys exercising authority and uses violence quite casually in order to ensure loyalty. He is also keen for the boys to believe in the beast, because he is the only one who can lead them in their fight against it as he says earlier: 'if there was a snake we'd hunt and kill it...' (p. 35).

Jack says that the beast cannot be killed and he resists attempts to link Simon's death to the defeat of the

> **Pause for thought**
>
> In Chapter 5 Jack accuses Ralph of telling them what to do without justification, 'Just giving orders that don't make sense' (p. 98) but now he punishes Wilfred for no apparent reason. How else does Jack begin to show he is a tyrant and a ruthless dictator?

beast. Jack plans to steal fire from Ralph as he has no means to start a fire himself. Meanwhile, Ralph, Piggy, Sam and Eric are struggling to keep the fire alight. They are now prepared to admit that the fire has a dual purpose, both as a beacon for passing ships and as a comfort in the dark.

Key quotation

This was the first time he had admitted the double function of the fire. Certainly one was to send up a beckoning column of smoke; but the other was to be a hearth now and a comfort until they slept.

(p. 179)

This second purpose has become increasingly important and Piggy has to remind Ralph that the fire means rescue.

While Ralph is dreaming of home, Jack leads an attack on the shelter, which collapses. After a confused fight in the darkness, Jack and his hunters make off with Piggy's glasses.

Chapter 11 Castle Rock

- Ralph and the three boys visit Jack.
- Ralph challenges Jack.
- Roger sends down a rock that kills Piggy.
- Sam and Eric are captured.
- The tribe attacks Ralph.

Key quotation

'They blinded me. See?' (p. 187)

Key quotation

'I'm going to that Jack Merridew an' tell him. I am.'

'You'll get hurt.'

'What can he do more than he has?'

(p. 189)

Key quotation

The rock struck Piggy a glancing blow from chin to knee; the conch exploded into a thousand white fragments and ceased to exist.

(p. 200)

Ralph says he would have given Jack fire but now it has been stolen from them. Piggy is practically blind without his glasses.

Piggy still thinks that appealing to Jack's sense of 'what's right's right' will work, so the four boys decide to go to see Jack.

There are now two very different forms of leadership on the island: Ralph wants to make life better for everyone and be rescued. Jack is turning more savage by the day, enjoying the power and freedom from civilised restraint that the absence of adults has given him.

Ralph, Piggy, Sam and Eric approach Castle Rock, hoping to reason with Jack. Jack appears from the forest and Ralph tells him he is a thief. The two fight and Sam and Eric are taken prisoner. In the excitement, Roger uses the lever to send the large rock crashing down on Piggy, knocking him off the causeway to the rocks far below. Piggy's body is swept out to sea.

The tribe attacks Ralph, who is wounded by a spear but manages to escape. Jack is

Grade *booster*

The following comment is likely from an A* candidate: 'Roger is typical of a weak person who is given great power. By hiding behind Jack he can exercise the kind of power that would never have been possible for him before. Roger also seems to enjoy violence: he shows no remorse over the fact that he has just killed Piggy. In many respects Roger resembles some of Hitler's henchmen, who were able to commit atrocities in the name of the Führer and Nazism.'

furious that Sam and Eric came to him carrying spears and that they did not join his tribe.

The twins try to reason with him, but the chapter closes with Roger moving menacingly towards them.

Key quotation

Roger advanced upon them as one wielding a nameless authority.

(p. 202)

Chapter 12 Cry of the hunters

- Ralph is alone in the forest.
- Jack hunts Ralph.
- The forest is set on fire.
- Ralph is chased to the beach.
- A naval officer appears on the beach.
- The boys are rescued.

Ralph sees the pig's head, now reduced to a white skull still on its stick, and lashes out at it. His action can be seen as symbolic. In destroying the pig's head he has smashed the idea of giving offerings to the beast. Ralph still retains his sense of right and wrong.

Key quotation

The skull regarded Ralph like one who knows all the answers and won't tell.

(p. 205)

Ralph sees Sam and Eric on top of the hill and approaches them. The twins tell Ralph that the tribe is going to hunt him in the morning, walking in a line across the island. It becomes apparent that the twins are even more afraid of Roger than of Jack. Although Jack is still the tribe's leader, Roger takes a sadistic pleasure in torture. In anticipation of catching Ralph, he has sharpened a stick at both ends, like the one used for the pig's head — a clear indication that he does not expect Ralph to live.

Key quotation

'You don't know Roger. He's a terror.'

(p. 210)

Ralph's hideout is discovered the next morning and Jack orders boulders to be pushed down on him.

Jack has the undergrowth set alight in order to burn Ralph out. Ralph realises time is running out.

At the last point of the island that is not ablaze Ralph collapses on the beach where they had first set up camp. He looks up to find a naval officer who has come because of the smoke from the fire. The officer assumes that the boys are playing games and jokingly says, 'What have you been doing? Having a war or something?' (p. 223).

The officer is surprised that a group of British boys has not been more organised and responsible.

Pause for thought

It is ironic that the fire that is used to force Ralph into the open is also the reason that the boys are rescued. At their most savage moment, the boys bring about an encounter with civilisation. Do you think this is just a good twist to the plot or does Golding intend to convey a message here? If so, what?

Key quotation

'I should have thought that a pack of British boys...would have been able to put up a better show than that'

(p. 224)

Ralph tries to explain that it started out like that, and the officer encouragingly refers to 'Coral Island'. This mention of Ballantyne's story, which shows ideal rather than realistic behaviour, takes us back to the seemingly innocent beginning of Golding's novel. It also reveals the limitations of the officer's thinking. Ralph breaks down in tears and the novel ends with the officer looking in embarrassment at the Navy ship lying offshore, unable to cope with this very un-British display of emotion.

> **Key quotation**
>
> Ralph wept for the end of innocence, the darkness of man's heart, and the fall through the air of the true, wise friend called Piggy.
>
> (p. 225)

The passage of time

Golding is deliberately vague about the timescale of the novel. Some events happen close together in time but days or even weeks might pass between other events.

Take the example of the dead parachutist. When he lands on the island he has obviously come from a plane that is shot up over the island. Although we are not told anything about how long he is there before Sam and Eric find him, by the time Ralph discovers the body it has 'the ruin of a face'. Of course this could be due to the body's being burnt as the plane exploded but it could equally be the result of its having rotted in the tropical heat. We do not know.

Think about how quickly the boys' clothes become torn and fall apart and how their hair grows long. How long does your hair take to grow? There are several examples of time passing quickly in the novel.

Timeline

Chapter	What happens	Timing
1	Ralph is made leader. The conch becomes a symbol of power	The events of these chapters take place on the first day on the island after the crash
2	One of the younger boys has seen a 'beastie'. The signal fire is lit on the mountain but gets out of control	
3	Jack hunts while Ralph focuses on building shelters	By now Jack has made a spear and is turning into a hunter. Ralph is building shelters. Some days or even weeks have passed

Chapter	What happens	Timing
4	A ship passes but the signal fire has gone out. Jack and Ralph argue and Piggy's glasses are broken in one eye. The hunters have killed a pig and there is a feast	The boys have been on the island for some time and have got used to 'the slow swing from dawn to quick dusk'
5	Fear of the beast grows. Ralph sees that order is breaking down. Jack defies Ralph and the conch	Later the same day as Chapter 4
6	The dead parachutist lands on the island. Sam and Eric hear the beast and report it	Some time has passed. The morning Sam and Eric see the dead airman may be some time after the body lands, not the next day
7	The hunters become more savage and the game gets dangerous. Jack and Ralph find the body and think it is the beast	Enough time has passed since the start of Chapter 6 for the body of the airman to have decomposed
8	Jack sets up his own tribe. The pig's head is left as a gift to the beast. Simon has a vision of the Lord of the Flies	Chapter 8 opens shortly after the discovery of the dead airman, probably the next day
9	The storm breaks. Simon is killed. The airman is blown out to sea	The storm has been developing for some time
10	Jack's tribe moves to Castle Rock. It attacks Ralph and his group and steals Piggy's glasses	This chapter opens the morning after Simon's death
11	Ralph's group visits Jack. Piggy is killed. The twins are captured	Chapter 11 opens straight after the attack on the camp by Jack's tribe — Eric is still covered in blood
12	Ralph is hunted. The island burns. The naval officer rescues the boys	Shortly after Piggy's death. Ralph spends one night in hiding before the hunt begins. The naval officer arrives at the end of the day

Grade *focus*

In the examination you will not be expected to write narrative accounts of what happens in the novel, but you will be expected to explore the events that occur.

Grade C answers:
- answer the question throughout
- refer to the novel all the way through and make comments on Golding's ideas
- use textual details, including quotations, all the way through
- explain the effects of the language, form or structure that Golding uses
- make some appropriate comments on themes, ideas or settings

Grade A* answers:

- make insightful comments on the text and the question

This might be something interesting about the leadership qualities of Ralph and Jack and what Golding is saying in the novel.

- look closely at the text and analyse detail to support the interpretation

This might be exploring the role of the fire at a specific moment and then comparing this to another detailed moment.

- evaluate the writer's uses of language and/or structure and/or form and the effects on readers

This might include an evaluation of the use of some of the symbols Golding exploits to show the darker side of humankind and nature in the novel.

- include a convincing and/or imaginative interpretation of ideas, themes or settings

This might be an exploration of the setting of the island as microcosm, reflecting the struggle for leadership going on in the outside world.

Review your learning

(Answers are given on p. 91.)

❶ Sum up the ten most important events of the novel.

❷ How are Piggy and Simon important to the plot?

❸ How is the relationship between Ralph and Jack central to the novel?

❹ How does the ending of the novel reflect the opening?

More interactive questions and answers online.

Characterisation

- What is each character like?
- What does each character want?
- What are the relationships between characters?
- How does Golding reveal the characters to us?
- What evidence can we find to help us think about each character?
- How will you be assessed?

It is important to note when writing your answer that it is impossible to separate the author's use of characterisation from the themes of the novel. The examples given below integrate both characters and themes throughout.

Ralph

Golding intended us to see him as the central character and gives him a decidedly heroic appearance. Ralph is fair-haired and stronger than the other boys, apart from Jack.

He is physically attractive and has a natural air of authority. In Chapter 1 Piggy looks at 'Ralph's golden body': his physical appearance is clearly a major factor in the other boys' seeing him as someone to follow.

There are early indications that Ralph is capable of at least limited cruelty. He cannot help himself from laughing at Piggy's school nickname and persists in calling him by the one name he has been asked not to use. Although Ralph is later capable of deciding between reason and instinct, he shows here that he is not so far from the later behaviour of Jack and that he certainly has this instinctive side to his personality.

Ralph also reveals that he is quite childlike when he talks of his father. He refers to him as 'Daddy', which is quite informal in front of another boy, and has a childlike faith in his father's powers.

Perhaps because Ralph has his father as a role model, being in charge seems to come easily to him: 'he found he could talk fluently and explain what he had to say' (p. 30). It is significant that it is Ralph who finds the conch. Though the shell eventually loses its importance, Ralph discovers the means of

> ### Key quotation
>
> **You could see now that he might make a boxer, as far as width and heaviness of shoulders went, but there was a mildness about his mouth and eyes that proclaimed no devil.** (p. 5)

> ### Grade *booster*
>
> A higher-band answer may comment on how Golding has simplified the situation on the island by creating only two characters who are nearly adolescents, while the rest are obviously still children. This means that the issue of leadership is fought out as a straight contest between Ralph and Jack.

> ### Key quotation
>
> **'He's a commander in the Navy. When he gets leave he'll come and rescue us.'** (p. 8)

...he was big enough
to be a link with
the adult world of
authority...   (p. 61)

Ralph holding the conch in
the 1990 film adaptation

Orion Pictures/pictorialpress.com

summoning the others and of establishing order in the early days of life on the island. This is linked with the idea of his being a natural leader. At the suggestion that the group ought to have a chief, Ralph does not immediately put himself forward. He does not react strongly to Jack's insistence that he himself ought to be chief because of his former status but simply lets the boys decide for themselves. This shows that Ralph is going to become a leader who values the opinions of others and who is likely to act in the best interests of the group.

Once the meetings start, he establishes himself as the boy to be listened to. He does not always know what to say, however, and often needs the help of Piggy to put into words what he is thinking. Ralph wants to organise the boys into building huts, keeping a supply of clean water and seeing that the fire is kept alight. Although Ralph is not a natural thinker at the start of the novel, he learns to appreciate that thought is a valuable thing. In Chapter 5 he shows he is becoming more of a thinker:

Once more that evening Ralph had to adjust his values. Piggy could think. He could go step by step inside that fat head of his, only Piggy was no chief. But Piggy, for all his ludicrous body, had brains. Ralph was a specialist in thought now, and could recognize thought in another.

(p. 83)

Ralph tries to be democratic even when dealing with the silliest things. For example he asks the boys to vote on whether or not the beast might be a ghost. This shows he lacks experience of being in authority. Ralph does not always do the strongest thing and at times falls back on the wishes of the group when he would do better to assert his own will.

For a time Ralph is able to control the boys by clever use of questions such as: 'don't any of you want to be rescued?' (p. 111), but he becomes frustrated when Jack begins to break away from the group.

Grade *booster*

High-level exam answers on Ralph will show an understanding that he represents a type of authority as well as being a character in the novel. Ralph would like to rule in the best interests of the group and would like the boys to behave reasonably. He is let down by this approach. Think what Golding is saying here about people who govern in the way that Ralph does. Letting reason rule may be a good idea, but not all people are reasonable.

He knows how to play on the fears of the other boys in such a way that they forget what Jack says about hunting. In Chapter 7 Ralph thinks about the life he enjoyed in England. He finds it comforting to slip back into memories of his early childhood. This seems normal enough but one cannot imagine Jack doing it. In this sense, Ralph remains rooted in civilised society, while Jack adapts more readily to their new situation and exploits it for his own ends.

Primitive impulses are always there in Ralph, as they are in Jack and the other boys, but Ralph usually manages to control this side of his nature, thanks to his well developed sense of morality.

> **Pause for thought**
>
> What would be your response to Ralph's question? Why does Jack hate him?

Ralph does not really understand why Jack is so much against him.

Ralph and Jack challenge each other to feats of bravery in front of the other boys and Ralph shows he is as strong as Jack. It is Ralph who decides they should make the final trip to see what it is that Sam and Eric have spotted on the mountain and at this point Ralph is very brave and clearly very strong willed.

Once Jack has left and taken most of the boys with him, Ralph starts to lose power and status. He looks a pitiful character in Chapter 9, when he approaches Jack's camp for meat.

Ralph is involved in the killing of Simon. This shows that the primitive side of his nature is stronger than he realises: to some extent he is in denial rather than simply being in control.

However, Ralph understands what he has done and shows moral courage in not letting Piggy disguise the killing as an accident. He sees that the only hope for survival is to be rescued.

Ralph puts his faith in the adult world to save the boys. When he decides to visit Jack in Chapter 11 he insists that Piggy, Sam and Eric put on their school uniforms to show that 'we aren't savages' (p. 189).

Even when he is fighting with Jack he uses phrases such as 'You aren't playing the game'. Ralph's sense of British fair play is an important aspect of his character. These words from Chapter 11 sum up Ralph's attitude:

> **Key quotation**
>
> 'Which is better, law and rescue, or hunting and breaking things up?'
>
> (p. 200)

Ralph survives only because of the arrival of the naval officer. His ideas of reason would not have held out against the savagery of Jack and Roger.

> **Key quotation**
>
> 'The rules!...you're breaking the rules!'
>
> (p. 99)

> **Key quotation**
>
> 'Why do you hate me?'
>
> (p. 129)

> **Key quotation**
>
> 'I'm chief. I'll go. Don't argue.'
>
> (p. 114)

> **Key quotation**
>
> The air was heavy with unspoken knowledge.
>
> (p. 175)

Jack

Jack can instil loyalty in some of the other boys. Jack and the choir are still wearing black cloaks and caps in the heat.

Key quotation

Inside the floating cloak he was tall, thin, and bony: and his hair was red beneath the black cap. His face was crumpled and freckled, and ugly without silliness. (p. 16)

Key quotation

'Choir! Stand still!'
(p. 16)

The colour black is symbolically important — Ralph is golden but Jack is black. Jack also likes the whole business of dressing up and playing a part. From the first, he treats the choir as a private army and clearly thinks in aggressive, military terms.

The choir calls him by his surname, Merridew. This formal use of surnames was common in boys' schools of this time.

Key quotation

'I ought to be chief... because I'm chapter chorister and head boy. I can sing C sharp.'
(p. 18)

On Roger's suggestion in Chapter 1 that there should be a chief, Jack instantly says he should be chief. This remark shows he can be vain and that he does not always think clearly before speaking or acting. The ability to sing C sharp might be impressive in a choir but is not a useful talent for life on the island.

We see an early indication of Jack's bluntness when he tells Piggy not to accompany him, Ralph and Simon on a tour of the area in order to see whether they are on an island: '"We don't want you," said Jack, flatly' (p. 21)

Pause for thought

Jack is 'ugly' and ends up bad; Ralph is 'golden' and ends up good. Do you think Golding believed you could judge from appearances? Do the boys choose their roles or are they forced into them? Remember that Golding is establishing his novel as a classic adventure story before gradually moving away from the traditions of the genre.

Key quotation

'Like in the war. You know – dazzle paint. Like things trying to look like something else'
(p. 66)

His head is full of ideas of hunting and he thinks this will be enough 'until they fetch us' (p. 27). Jack reveals his selfishness here and also his lack of ability to think very far ahead. He has no thought for the weaker members of the group and embodies the notion of survival of the fittest.

In Chapter 4 he paints his face and it is as though the child in Jack is replaced by a primitive hunter: 'The mask compelled them' (p. 67).

In the same chapter, Jack rejoices at killing the pig even though his hunters have let the fire go out and the boys have missed the chance to attract a passing ship. There is a mixture of the savage and the child in Jack and we see the child who likes to play gradually being replaced by the primitive hunter.

Jack increasingly combats Ralph's democratic rules.

At the end of Chapter 6 Jack discovers the 'fort'. He seems to be quite childish about the idea of playing soldiers but at the same time there is something sinister in his desire to shut himself away in a fortress. Jack wants to behave like a king who rules his kingdom from his castle and uses fear to control his subjects.

In Chapter 7 Jack leads the attack on Robert and uses his spear on the other boy, whipping the hunters into a frenzy and suggesting at the end of the attack that they should act the kill out properly.

Jack confronts Ralph

Jack shows he can be devious when he claims that Ralph hadn't gone to the top of the mountain to find the beast (Chapter 8). When Jack decides to break away from the group his words are a strange mixture of strength and childishness (Chapter 8).

> **Key quotation**
>
> 'I'm going off by myself. He can catch his own pigs. Anyone who wants to hunt when I do can come too.'   (p. 140)

Jack elects himself chief and finds that the others will do whatever he says — not a good thing given Jack's tendency to be cruel. Jack has the idea of leaving a sacrifice for the beast and loves the bloodiness of the kill. He leaves the pig's head as an offering and so is indirectly responsible for the effect this has on Simon.

Chapter 9 has a strong image that shows Jack's power. Jack is standing at the feast giving orders to the other boys. He appears like a king or tribal chief.

In the eyes of the other boys, Jack is now more powerful than Ralph. The fact that he can bring them meat when Ralph can only talk of the fire and rescue gives him this power.

> **Key quotation**
>
> ...painted and garlanded, sat there like an idol.
>
> (p. 164)

Grade *booster* !

Stronger answers might comment on the fact that, even though Jack does not consciously set out to disturb Simon, it is Jack's actions that lead to Simon's death. Jack sets the pig's head on a stick and it is this that causes Simon to have his fit and then to come stumbling into the group of boys.

Key quotation

'See? See? That's what you'll get! I meant that! There isn't a tribe for you any more! The conch is gone...'

(p. 201)

Jack uses the killing of Simon to increase his hold over the other boys. Jack's savage nature shows most clearly when he is facing Ralph in Chapter 11. Jack is quite prepared to kill Ralph.

The final hunt for Ralph results in a fire that will have destroyed all the food on the island. Jack does not think about this, because his sole interest is in killing Ralph. Once Ralph had been killed, Jack would have had to pick another boy to fight against because he needs an enemy with which to threaten the other boys.

Pause for thought

Ralph and Jack are very different characters. What are the main differences between them and what is Golding trying to say by making them so different?

Piggy

Piggy is presented by Golding as a weak boy who has good ideas. The first time he appears in the novel he tells Ralph about his asthma. He is overweight and finds the climate of the island especially difficult.

Grade booster

It is important that Piggy is not physically strong so he cannot be leader. To achieve a high grade you could comment on how Golding has chosen to make the most intelligent boy also one of the weakest. This is deliberate and shows that being clever is not always enough and that appearance is overvalued.

Key quotation

'My auntie told me not to run...on account of my asthma...and I've been wearing specs since I was three.'

(p. 3)

We find out very early that Piggy, despite his intelligence, is also gullible (easily taken in). He tells Ralph that he doesn't want to be called Piggy. This is an obvious mistake and it is clear that he is not going to command respect from the other boys.

Key quotation

'I got to have them specs. Now I only got one eye.'

(p. 76)

Grade booster

Consider what Golding is saying about people like Piggy. Although the boys need his wisdom for their long-term survival, they cast him aside quite early on. Because he cannot back his ideas up with force, Piggy is unable to influence events on the island once Jack becomes powerful. You should be prepared to comment on the relationship Golding is exploring here between brute strength and intelligence.

It is significant that Piggy's glasses are used to light the fire, which gives him some importance — even to Jack. Piggy's short-sightedness helps to make him a figure of fun to the other boys, but his glasses can be seen as a symbol of his intellectual vision and of civilisation itself. As Piggy's glasses deteriorate, so does Piggy, and so do the fortunes of the boys.

As early as Chapter 2, unthinking behaviour by the group causes problems for Piggy. He is horrified that the boys have started a forest fire, as he realises it means the destruction of their wood supply.

Golding connects Piggy to the world of humans and human progress. Think about the number of times Piggy mentions human inventions such as clocks and radios. Golding's point is that the trappings of civilised life are of little use on the island.

It is important to realise that Piggy represents a particular type of person and way of doing things. Piggy is a thinker, capable of taking the rough ideas that Jack and Ralph have and shaping them into plans for action.

Piggy appears weak and does not naturally command attention. He repeats himself and sounds ridiculous — as in his repeated cries of 'I got the conch' (e.g. p. 172). Gradually, by association, his ideas sound ridiculous too. Piggy lacks imagination, wit or charisma.

Piggy instinctively seeks Ralph's protection from Jack's bullying. Gradually the two become closer and depend on each other.

> **Key quotation**
>
> 'In a year or two when the war's over they'll be travelling to Mars and back. I know there isn't no beast – not with claws and all that, I mean – but I know there isn't no fear, either.' (p. 90)

Piggy's loyalty and his death

Piggy remains loyal to Ralph until the very end. He has seen that Jack is nothing but a bully. It is reasonable to assume that Piggy has met boys such as Jack before. Even though Ralph teases Piggy, this is taken as normal behaviour. Piggy knows that without Ralph's protection he would be Jack's victim.

At the moment of his death Piggy is still holding up the conch. He still seems to think that the early rule about the holder of the conch being allowed to speak will be respected by the likes of Roger. When Roger levers the boulder over the edge it kills Piggy and destroys the conch. Thus the voice and the symbol of reason are destroyed together. This is a particularly cowardly act, as Piggy poses no real threat to Jack or Roger. It is simply a case of the strong attacking the weak. With the death of Piggy, Ralph is alone. He has no one to advise him and the importance of Piggy's ability to think straight becomes ever clearer.

Ralph with Piggy

Orion Pictures/pictorialpress.com

Pause for thought

Golding may be suggesting that Piggy's treatment is typical of how thinkers are treated. Some people resent those who are clever. Others, such as Ralph, realise the value of thinkers. Piggy is laughed at when he first comes up with an idea but, shortly after, his idea becomes the plan of action for all the boys. His physical appearance and weakness cause the others to dismiss him. Can you think of parallels in society for the way in which he is treated? Can you see how the main characters in the novel represent certain groups of people in society?

Simon

Simon is an unusual character. We learn in Chapter 1 that he regularly faints:

> **Key quotation**
>
> **'He's always throwing a faint,' said Merridew. 'He did in Gib.; and Addis; and at matins over the precentor.'** (p. 16)

Here Golding depicts the typical reaction of children to anything unusual in others. Simon is looked upon as being odd because he suffers from something that the other boys do not understand. When we finally get to see how one of Simon's attacks affects him, it seems likely that he is suffering from some form of epilepsy and that he is not simply fainting. Simon is described as:

> **Key quotation**
>
> **a skinny, vivid little boy, with a glance coming up from under a hut of straight hair that hung down, black and coarse.** (p. 20)

It is clear that he is no physical match for Ralph or Jack. Yet, in spite of his apparent weakness, he has a certain presence. This can be seen when Ralph decides that Simon should come with him and Jack to explore the island.

Simon is capable of having good practical ideas. He suggests they make a map on tree bark because there is no paper (Chapter 1). He is also a kind boy: when Piggy is accused in Chapter 2 of being useless, it is Simon who points out that Piggy's glasses were used to start the fire.

Simon is loyal to Ralph. He is the only boy who helps Ralph build the first shelters, but even Ralph finds Simon odd: 'he's funny' (p. 56).

Simon goes off on his own without warning. In Chapter 3 he leaves Ralph and Jack and goes into the forest. The young boys follow him and he finds them food. This image of Simon as a leader of the simple children and provider of food for them has clear parallels with the New Testament accounts of Jesus and his followers. Other biblical parallels involving Simon occur in the plot.

> **Pause for thought**
>
> Do you think Simon is more involved with fact (there is no beast) or vision ('his inward sight')? Golding surrounds Simon with some of the most poetic language in the novel. What do you think he is saying about the role of religion in society?

The account of his trip into the forest at the end of Chapter 3 is full of almost religious imagery, and Simon seems to have a mystical quality about him. However, he is quick to counter his involvement in the creation

 PHILIP ALLAN LITERATURE GUIDE **FOR GCSE**

of the beast myth. When some of the small boys say they are worried about the beast, Simon admits that he has gone into the forest alone at night.

Simon makes the radical suggestion that the beast exists in the boys themselves — an idea that is too difficult for the other boys to grasp and that only makes them laugh at him. He is the only boy who is really aware of the dark side that each boy has. After Sam and Eric have seen the dead airman, only Simon thinks it is unlikely that there really is a beast.

In Chapter 6 Simon thinks there is an injured human on the mountain, and he is very nearly right. He has a much clearer insight into this question, and the boys' situation on the island as a whole, than the rest of the group. Golding thus conveys the idea that Simon sees things that the others do not see. Even though this is not really supernatural, it would seem that way to the boys.

Simon suggests that they should all climb the mountain and face the beast. His mystical side becomes very important in Chapter 8, when he watches the pig's head on the stick. He imagines the 'Lord of the Flies' speaking to him and telling him that he is a 'silly little boy'. The vision also tells him that he was right to think that the beast was part of him and the others. Again, note the biblical overtones in this scene (it parallels the story of Jesus being tempted by the devil in the wilderness).

The final warning that Simon imagines turns out to be horribly appropriate. He imagines the beast saying: 'we shall do you. See? Jack and Roger and Maurice and Robert and Bill and Piggy and Ralph. Do you. See?' (p. 159)

Simon recovers from his fit and frees the dead airman (Chapter 9). He then sets off to find the others and tell them that the beast is nothing to be afraid of. When he bursts into the circle of boys he tries to tell them about the dead man on the hill, but he is killed before he can deliver his message properly.

Simon also has much in common with the stories of saints who saw strange visions. Many saints were misunderstood and even persecuted for their unusual ideas. Even the name 'Simon' is the same as that of one of Christ's followers, Simon the Zealot, who was martyred: some stories have him crucified, others sawn in half. Simon mirrors his death closely. Like the Zealot, Simon is a visionary who can see beyond 'belief systems' to Golding's truth that good and evil exist within us and that the only beast we fear is the potential for evil inside us. He could also represent the most important of Christ's disciples. Simon was called 'Peter' by Jesus; the name Peter comes from the Latin word for rock. Simon Peter was the first pope and therefore the first leader of the Christian church.

Key quotation

> Simon became inarticulate in his effort to express mankind's essential illness. Inspiration came to him.
>
> 'What's the dirtiest thing there is?'
>
> (p. 96)

Key quotation

> 'I just *think you'll get back all right*'
>
> (p. 121)

Read the passage from 'Simon, walking in front of Ralph' to 'the chief would have to go forward' (Chapter 6, p. 112).

Here, instead of using the boys' speech to reveal their feelings, Golding has chosen to focus on a description of their thoughts and actions. This is necessary in order to give the reader an insight into Simon, because he says less than the other boys. In this passage we see that Simon has a wisdom that sets him apart from the others. He is sceptical about the beast, on the basis of the evidence. However, his image of 'a human at once heroic and sick' — which turns out to describe the pilot that the boys mistake for the beast — could be said to derive from a sixth sense. One could say that Simon is clairvoyant.

He somehow senses the truth without having to see evidence.

In the second paragraph, Golding is still writing in the third person, but from Simon's viewpoint. Hence it is Simon who feels 'that dreadful feeling of the pressure of personality'. This is not meant to be an objective description of how it feels for all boys to speak in public.

We see that, despite Simon's wisdom and vision (or perhaps because of them), he is an outsider. Even Ralph only tolerates him. When Simon walks into a tree, making Ralph dismiss him and Robert laugh at him, we see that Simon's wisdom does not necessarily help him to cope with the material world. How do you respond to Simon's walking into the tree, and to Ralph's response?

Roger

We first begin to see his character emerge in Chapter 4. Some of the smaller boys have built sandcastles and spent time decorating them with shells, flowers and stones. Roger comes out of the forest after watching the fire and immediately kicks the sandcastles over. He has no reason to do this; it is done simply out of badness.

Also in Chapter 4 we see Roger enjoying teasing Henry, a young boy. Roger throws stones all round Henry but hides behind a tree each time. For Roger this is not so much a game as a practice for the kind of person he is going to become.

In the presence of Jack, who arrives following the teasing, Roger changes and becomes darker still.

After the mock hunt in Chapter 7, Roger seems genuinely disappointed

Key quotation

...unsociable remoteness into something forbidding.

(Description of Roger, p. 63)

Key quotation

Roger's arm was conditioned by a civilization that knew nothing of him and was in ruins.

(p. 65)

Key quotation

When Roger opened his eyes and saw him, a darker shadow crept beneath the swarthiness of his skin.

(p. 65)

Grade booster

Golding does not give many physical descriptions of Roger. He looks simply dark and brooding. You could comment that this might be a deliberate ploy to make Roger seem mysterious and threatening.

that the violence has not gone far enough and wishes they had a real pig to kill. Roger accompanies Ralph and Jack in the search for the beast. On this expedition he does not say much but is a brooding presence throughout.

In Chapter 8 Roger helps to kill the pig. This is not done quickly: 'The spear moved forward inch by inch and the terrified squealing became a high-pitched scream' (p. 149). It is not a coincidence that it is Roger who carries out this cruel act. Roger learns from Jack the importance of terror as a means of control.

> **Key quotation**
>
> Roger, uncommunicative by nature, said nothing. He offered no opinion on the beast nor told Ralph why he had chosen to come on this mad expedition.
>
> (pp. 132–33)

Grade *booster*

Consider what Golding is using Roger for. He likes to be involved in dangerous escapades but doesn't show any real interest. He is an evil element that is present whenever any of the boys shows weakness. Roger symbolises the destructive side of human nature that takes pleasure in the suffering of others.

In Chapter 8 he follows Jack's orders and sharpens a stick at both ends to display the pig's head. In the final hunt for Ralph it is Roger's own idea to sharpen a stick at both ends.

A major turning point in the development of Roger's character comes in Chapter 10. He learns that Wilfred has been tied up by Jack and is going to be beaten. No one seems to know what Wilfred has done, but Roger sees this as an exciting opportunity.

This is the point at which Roger realises that power creates opportunities for terror. He has no real interest in the outcome of the terror but is simply fascinated by the idea of being able to hurt others without being stopped.

The most defining point in Roger's character comes in Chapter 11 when he kills Piggy. He is very excited by the fight between Ralph and Jack and feels the need to join in.

> **Key quotation**
>
> Roger received this news as an illumination. He... sat still, assimilating the possibilities of irresponsible authority.
>
> (p. 176)

> **Key quotation**
>
> High overhead, Roger, with a sense of delirious abandonment, leaned all his weight on the lever.
>
> (p. 200)

Grade *booster*

Roger can be seen to represent a part of human nature that is present in everyone. The rules of society cause most people to keep this side of their nature under control. Roger has no one to stop him so he goes much further than he could at home. He is an example of the evil side of human nature let loose, something that higher-mark answers might explore.

This 'delirious abandonment' is a development of the idea that Roger can have power without responsibility. He kills Piggy when there is absolutely no need. This is simply bullying carried as far as it can go. The final indication of his cruelty is the moment when he comes down from

the cliff to look at what he has done to Piggy. Even Jack backs away from him because, as Golding describes:

> **Key quotation**
>
> **The hangman's horror clung to him.** (p. 202)

Not only has he killed Piggy but he wants to admire his handiwork.

It is Roger who terrifies Sam and Eric into joining Jack's tribe. When Ralph meets the twins in the final chapter Sam tells him: 'You don't know Roger. He's a terror' (p. 210). Finally, the twins tell Ralph that Roger has 'sharpened a stick at both ends' (p. 211). The significance of this is clear, as the last time this was done, the stick was put into the ground and used to display the pig's severed head. Even killing Ralph is not enough for Roger; he wants to be able to put Ralph's head on a stick.

> **Key quotation**
>
> **...Roger who carried death in his hands?** (p. 218)

Roger may be the only character who poses a threat to Jack:

> **Key quotation**
>
> **Roger advanced upon them as one wielding a nameless authority.** (p. 202)

He barely misses barging into Jack, showing there is a possible threat present.

Sam and Eric

The twins Sam and Eric are loyal to Ralph until the final episode. They spot the dead airman but are too afraid to investigate and so help to build up the myth of the beast.

The twins are important as symbols of the kind of sensible follower that a leader such as Ralph would rely on. They are never persuaded by Jack's style of leadership and join his tribe only because they are threatened and tortured by Roger. Even so, their change of allegiance comes as a serious blow to Ralph.

It is particularly striking that, when Ralph is hunted by Jack in Chapter 12, it is Sam and Eric who betray his hiding place.

> **Key quotation**
>
> **Samneric were savages like the rest; Piggy was dead, and the conch smashed to powder.** (p. 207)

> **Pause for thought**
>
> What is your personal response to Sam and Eric's betrayal of Ralph? Consider the possible parallels, such as in Nazi Germany, where people with no real sympathy for the Nazis were persuaded, by threats, to betray Jews or others regarded as enemies of the state. You may be able to think of examples closer to home.

The other boys

Robert, Maurice, Percival and Henry are examples of the general population of the island. They are happy to follow Ralph to begin with. Some feel loyalty to Jack through the choir. In the end they are all won over by Jack's love of hunting or by his ability to frighten them into submission.

The main group of boys represents the general population of any society. The little ones are very easily persuaded and will go along with whichever leader makes them follow him. They change sides quickly and easily and often make poor decisions about who is right and who is wrong.

Golding uses the non-central characters to suggest the way in which groups of people behave. He clearly feels that many people in society are easily led. Remember that he had just fought in a war against normal people who had followed a cruel and fanatical leader.

The island burns

Orion Pictures/pictorialpress.com

Grade *focus*

Questions will often ask you to look at one character and to comment on his role in the novel. You may be asked:

> Is Jack an effective leader in the novel?
>
> What role does Piggy have in *Lord of the Flies*?

For more details see the *Sample essays* section on p. 78.

Grades G–D

In this range of grades, candidates' answers are likely to deal with the characters as real people only. There might well be detailed accounts of the actions of the boys and comments about certain boys being cruel, savage, and so on. At this level candidates will tend not to discuss the way in which different boys are created to help the writer illustrate his themes.

The better candidates in this grade range will support comments with references to the text.

Grades C–A*

In this grade range examiners will expect to see that you know about the actions of the boys (as above), but also that you realise that aspects of general human behaviour can be seen in certain boys. The best candidates will be able to discuss the characters equally as psychologically realistic and as creations to help the writer illustrate and explore his themes.

Review your learning

(Answers are given on p. 92.)

1. Select three quotations that illustrate the major character aspects of Ralph, Jack, Piggy and Simon.
2. What sort of a leader is Ralph?
3. What sort of leader is Jack?
4. Comment on the ways in which Ralph, Jack, Piggy and Simon change during the course of the novel.
5. Discuss the relationships between:

   a Ralph and Jack

   b Ralph and Piggy

   c Jack and Roger

   d Simon and Ralph

   e The older boys and the littluns

More interactive questions and answers online.

Themes

- **What is a theme?**
- **What are the main themes in *Lord of the Flies*?**
- **How do these themes relate to each other?**
- **How do these themes relate to the characters?**

A theme in a novel is an idea or group of ideas that the author explores. There is no absolutely correct way to define the themes in any novel, and in any interpretation of literary themes there is bound to be some overlap.

These are the main themes of *Lord of the Flies*:

- good versus evil
- the 'heart of darkness' in each one of us
- rules and society
- nature versus nurture (instinctive as opposed to learned behaviour)
- survival of the fittest
- fear of the beast
- human interaction with nature

You cannot cover all the themes in depth in an examination essay.

Good versus evil

On a first reading of *Lord of the Flies*, you may see this issue as a very simple matter: some of the boys' actions are good whereas others' are evil. However, the novel is actually more complex than that. Consider the examples in the table below.

Normally at any one time a boy's actions are driven by a mixture of good and evil and the central column in the table below contains the kinds of ideas that a top-level answer would include.

Grade *booster*

A* candidates might comment on how Golding makes several of the main characters much more complex than just good or evil. This reflects his interest in how people can move from being good to being evil. None of the boys (even Roger) is thoroughly evil when the novel starts.

Clearly good	Unclear	Clearly evil
Ralph builds shelters to help all the boys	Ralph tells the boys Piggy's nickname	Roger kills Piggy
Jack gives all the boys a share of the first pig he catches	Jack plays the hunting game with a real boy	Jack orders the death of Ralph

Pause for thought

Piggy is a good character in the novel. There is nothing really evil about him. Think of all the other boys in the novel. Who is essentially good, who is evil and who is neither? Can you find evidence to support your ideas?

There are forces acting on the boys that bring about changes in their characters. If there were a ready source of meat on the island then Jack would not become the savage hunter that he turns into. If the dead airman had not landed on the island then many of the fears about the beast would not have developed as far as they do. The novel traces the effects of such forces on different boys. There are real tests of character on the island. Some boys behave well under this pressure but others become cruel and primitive. The way in which different boys respond to pressure is a key feature of the novel.

The heart of darkness

The phrase 'heart of darkness' comes from a novel of this name by Joseph Conrad (published 1902). Conrad's novel is about a civilised man's descent into savagery. The central character, Kurtz, has been strongly affected by living in a remote part of Africa and has become a savage himself. This was a concern at the time, when European countries ruled over large areas of the world and saw themselves as 'civilised' and many of the countries they governed as 'primitive'. The fear that a person could find the native way of life attractive and begin to adopt it was real. (The word 'native' in this context did not necessarily mean primitive: 'going native' usually meant adopting the style of dress of the locals, eating local food and following local customs, although even this was considered eccentric. Even in hot countries, in Africa or Asia, you would have seen the British dressed as they would have been at home.)

In *Lord of the Flies* Golding explores the same idea as Conrad but focuses entirely on the European side of the equation. There are no savages to 'corrupt' the English, as there are in Conrad's story. Ralph and Piggy try to remain civilised whereas Jack and Roger become like primitive savages. Keeping up appearances and trying to be very 'British' about everything is part of what drives Ralph.

You will find the phrase 'the darkness of man's heart' on the last page of the novel. This is part of Ralph's thoughts on what has happened, and the wording Golding uses is not accidental.

Jack does not set out to become the wild savage that he eventually turns into. Rather, this happens in a series of small changes. Some of his behaviour might have been learned at school. For instance, he would have known that tribal people often painted themselves before a hunt or a battle. What he discovers on the island is that hunting is much more satisfactory if there is some ceremony attached to it. There is no need to dance or to develop rituals around the killing of a pig. This is something that comes from Jack himself.

The novel explores the idea that there are circumstances in which any individual could become a primitive human being who is driven by instinct. The dark side of human nature is strong in both Jack and Roger and they are not able to control where this takes them. They revert to a much more primitive form of behaviour than that of modern Western society. Golding is putting forward the idea that some people are more likely than others to let their primitive instincts rule them. Jack and the hunters become uncivilised in the wildest sense.

Primitive savages?

Alamy/Photos 12

Rules and society

At the start of the book the boys cling closely to things associated with their former life. They still wear their uniforms in spite of the heat. Jack still addresses the choir. Gradually these old ties to the adult world disappear. The boys' clothes fall apart and the hunters discard most of theirs and paint themselves instead.

Key quotation

> **The world, that understandable and lawful world,
> was slipping away.**
>
> (p. 98)

Grade *booster*

A* candidates might explore the fact that, like any teacher, Golding had seen at first hand that boys could be cruel to one another at the slightest provocation. In the novel he reveals what he thinks might happen to any typical group of boys once the normal rules of society are removed.

Ralph tries to run the island in the way that a British adult would have done. The conch, the shelters, rules about where to take water from and where to go to the toilet are all aspects of this. It is true that Ralph's and Piggy's ideas would probably have resulted in the best life for the whole group. It is also likely that, if the fire had been kept going as Ralph wanted, then the boys would have been rescued by the first ship.

Because there are no adults to enforce the rules, the society on the island gradually falls apart. The reason and interest in the common good that Ralph shows is overpowered by the primitive side of human nature that emerges in Jack and the hunters.

Grade *booster*

The novel explores the idea that children behave in a civilised way only because adults make them. Think about a typical bullying incident in a school. There are many times when such a situation would be much worse if there were no teachers and parents around to intervene.

Key quotation

Roger gathered a handful of stones and began to throw them. Yet there was a space round Henry... into which he dare not throw... Round the squatting child was the protection of parents and school and policemen and the law. (pp. 64–65)

At this stage Roger is still influenced by the rules of a civilised society, represented by parents, school, the police and the law but, by the end of the novel, this has been stripped away because none of these agencies is present on the island. Once the conch has been smashed, Piggy killed and the fire on the mountain quenched, even the symbolic representations of civilisation have disappeared and Roger can free the beast within him, without fear of recrimination. Golding shows that, if there is a threat to Jack as leader, it is Roger in his 'only just avoiding pushing' (p. 202) Jack out of the way in his advance upon Sam and Eric to show him the proper way to torture.

Key quotation

The officer...was moved and a little embarrassed. He turned away to give them time to pull themselves together...

(p. 225)

The end of the novel is significant with regard to this idea. It is an adult who comes to the rescue — an adult in authority. In the end the old world of rules and 'proper' behaviour returns to the lives of the boys. It is also significant that Golding does not tell us what happens to the boys once they are off the island. Would Jack have been punished? Would Roger have been made accountable? These questions are left unanswered. The novel is concerned with the closed world of the island and does not try to explain what society would have made of the boys' behaviour. The naval officer thinks that the boys have been playing a game. He does not realise how dangerous a game it has been. The adult world of rules cannot understand what the boys have been through.

Text **focus**

Read the passage in Chapter 11 from 'Piggy held up the shell' to 'you got to!' (pp. 189–90).

Here Piggy makes a moving and almost heroic plea for social justice. He accepts the indignity of having to be 'led like a dog' because of his poor eyesight. He sticks to his personal values, in which common sense and order rank above irrationality and savagery, and he demands rhetorically 'What's grown-ups goin' to think?' The fact that he is doomed, because the situation has moved beyond reason and order, is suggested by the line 'The shape of the old assembly, trodden in the grass, listened to him'. It is as if only ghosts from the past hear his words.

Read aloud Piggy's final speech in the passage. Notice the strong, simple words and rhythms he uses to present his heartfelt belief in what is right. What is your response to Piggy at this point?

Nature versus nurture

This debate is about whether a person is born good or evil (nature) or learns to be good or evil (nurture). It is an old question, which we find, for example, in Shakespeare. It was of great interest to the Victorians, and writers such as Dickens explored it in depth. Take the character of Nancy in *Oliver Twist*, who has been brought up on the streets and sold into prostitution while still a child. Even with this awful upbringing she sacrifices herself to save young Oliver.

Roger represents the type of person who is naturally evil and just needs a chance to let this evil run free. Golding leaves it open to the reader to decide why this is. We do not know what nurturing or lack of nurturing factors have made Jack and Roger the way they are.

The murder of Simon shows that even the boys who are good can be influenced to be evil. The key factor with Ralph and Piggy is their remorse for their part in the killing. Piggy tries to pretend it did not happen, but he is still sorry for Simon; Ralph talks about the incident and realises he has been part of something terrible.

Grade *booster*

Higher-grade candidates could explore how some philosophers believe that a person's nature cannot be changed. If someone is naturally evil, then all that person needs is an opportunity for this side of his or her nature to come out. Jack and Roger clearly have a greater tendency to be evil than many of the other boys.

Pause for thought

Ralph, Piggy, Simon, Sam and Eric tend to be good. What evidence can you find for the good nature of Ralph, Piggy, Simon, Sam and Eric? Why has Golding included more boys who have a tendency to good than those who have a tendency to be evil?

Key quotation

'You were outside. Outside the circle. You never really came in. Didn't you see what we – what they did?'

(p. 173)

Survival of the fittest

Charles Darwin introduced this idea as part of his work on the way species develop through evolution. According to Darwin's theory, species of creatures adapt to their surroundings over time, leading to the huge variety we see in life on earth. The creatures that are best suited to their environment (the fittest) have a greater chance of survival than weaker creatures or those less well adapted to their surroundings.

Examples from nature would be:

- in a nest, the strongest chicks attract the parents' attention the most effectively and so get the most food
- pups, kittens or cubs in a litter have to fight for food — the strongest ones get the most food while the weaker ones may die

Darwin gave many examples, including species of birds that had lost the ability to fly because they had become adapted to a place where there were no predators. He put forward the theory that creatures naturally choose the strongest and most successful mates and that the characteristics that make them successful are passed on down the generations.

Golding uses the notion of survival of the fittest in the novel. Ralph is clearly the best leader in terms of running things in a 'civilised' British way. In reality, this counts for nothing in the face of Jack's brutality, which makes Jack appear to be well suited to survival on the island (for one thing, he is a good hunter). While Jack is suited to his surroundings, Ralph tries to change the surroundings to suit himself.

However, although Jack comes close to killing Ralph and almost shows brutality to be more successful here than reason, he finally sets the island on fire. Jack and the other boys might well have starved after the fire, as they would have burnt down all the fruit trees. In the end Jack turns out to be no more of a true survivor than Ralph. Jack's instincts make him the stronger of the two leaders in the circumstances, but his need to destroy would probably have led to disaster for all the boys.

Fear of the beast

One of the forces driving the actions of the boys is the fear they have of the beast. This begins with some of the small boys being frightened by the jungle creepers that hang from the trees. It quickly develops into a fear of a beast that lives in the sea and comes out at night.

At the very point when the older boys are about to persuade the others that there is no beast, the dead airman confuses matters. Sam and Eric see the body on the mountain but do not investigate. Simon does find out what 'the beast' really is and cuts the cords from the rocks so that the

Grade *booster*

Golding does not allow Jack to win. You can earn higher marks by analysing the fact that this is part of the message of the book: that brute force will not triumph over intelligence.

Key quotation

'Which is better, law and rescue, or hunting and breaking things up?'

(Ralph, p. 200)

Pause for thought

Primo Levi stated that '…the fittest survived; the best all died'.

Consider the deaths of Piggy and Simon as well as the near death of Ralph. Does the 'fittest' mean the best in a moral sense or can it be, depending on the environment, the worst?

wind can take the body away. Tragically, he is killed in the circle before he can get his explanation out.

The beast in the novel is always referred to in naturalistic terms: it is a snake, it comes from the sea, it is a great ape. From the earliest records of humankind, cultures have taken images from the natural world in this way and created spirits, monsters, demons and gods. From the Egyptian animal gods to the Minotaur and the Christian devil, human societies tend to give their fears a solid form and a name.

Throughout human history religions have developed that help people to feel more secure in the world and less fearful. They have their own explanations of the mysterious things found in nature (such as birth, death, the seasons) and usually have elaborate rituals associated with them. Although a fully developed religion does not appear on the island, there are signs that the early stages of this are present.

> ### Key quotation
>
> **Simon became inarticulate in his effort to express mankind's essential illness.**
>
> (p. 96)

Grade *booster*

You might consider why the author lets the reader know that there is not a real beast on the island. The reader is always ahead of the boys on this. It is important that we know more than the characters so that the novel does not become a mystery tale or a horror story.

Text focus

In Chapter 8, the beast, who has played a prominent role in the novel so far, is represented by a pig's head on a stick, which Simon encounters alone. The following quotations are taken from the end of the chapter (pp. 157–59).

'You are a silly little boy,' said the Lord of the Flies, 'just an ignorant, silly little boy.'

'…you'd better run off and play with the others…'

There isn't anyone to help you. Only me. And I'm the Beast.

'Fancy thinking the Beast was something you could hunt and kill!' said the head…'You knew, didn't you? I'm part of you? Close, close, close! I'm the reason why it's no go? Why things are what they are?'

…obscene thing on a stick.
The Lord of the Flies was expanding like a balloon.

The Lord of the flies spoke in the voice of a schoolmaster.
'This has gone quite far enough. My poor, misguided child, do you think you know better than I do?'

Simon found he was looking into a vast mouth. There was blackness within, a blackness that spread.

Simon was inside the mouth.

How does Golding describe this encounter with the beast?

What would happen if Simon got to the other boys and told them about his discovery?

Humans and nature

The boys are provided with the perfect environment in which to survive. All they have to do is to make full use of the surroundings. At first they take delight in the fruit trees and nature really does seem to have given them all they need. The fact that there are pigs on the island causes conflict to arise. It is difficult to imagine Jack developing the same intense feelings about fruit picking.

Key quotation

The flames, as though they were a kind of wild life, crept as a jaguar creeps on its belly towards a line of birch-like saplings...

(p. 44)

Apart from one storm, on the night of Simon's death, even the weather is kind to the boys. They find it hot, but at least they do not have to worry about being cold at night. The natural surroundings could be said to be benign (meaning kind or forgiving). The boys need only to treat nature with respect and they will never go short of food.

The first fire destroys part of the island. This should be a warning to the boys but not all listen to it. Even with the knowledge that fire can devastate the island, Jack chooses to burn Ralph out.

Pause for thought

The behaviour of the boys towards their environment is typical of the way that humans have often treated the planet. Golding is aware that humankind is stupid enough to destroy the very land that gives it food and life. This fact has become more topical since the book was written. Do you think Golding intended to convey an environmental message in this novel?

The bloodlust that rises in Jack is uncontrollable. In the hunt for Ralph, Jack effectively destroys the things that nature has given the boys. This is an important idea in the book, and you should be able to draw parallels with the world at the time the novel was written. You could also extend this to ways in which the book remains relevant today.

Review your learning

(Answers are given on p. 93.)

1 What do you think are the main themes of the novel?

2 What wider issues is the author exploring through his use of these themes?

3 Why do you think Golding has chosen these particular themes?

4 How are the major themes explored through the characters?

5 What relevance do you think the themes of the novel have in today's world?

More interactive questions and answers online.

Style

- **To which features does the term 'style' refer?**
- **How does Golding use the setting of the island?**
- **What use does he make of description?**
- **How realistic is the dialogue?**
- **What viewpoint does the writer adopt?**
- **How does Golding use imagery and symbolism?**

In the examination, style includes looking at language, form and structure, which are key elements of Assessment Objective 2 (AO2) (see p. 71 for further details).

Reading the novel and being able to retell the story is a low-level skill, and you will not gain marks in the exam for doing this. You have to give examples from the novel to illustrate your comments, but you should not simply give an account of actions.

Style is the *way* that a writer expresses the ideas in the novel. When you write about style, you are showing that you understand an important fact: the author of a novel has numerous choices.

Golding has made choices about the following features covered by the word 'style':

- how the setting adds to the story
- how dialogue (conversation) is used and how realistic it is
- what description is included: for example, adjectives describing a character's appearance and adverbs describing how someone speaks
- the viewpoint from which the story is told: especially whether it is third person ('Ralph turned to the sea') or first person (told through the speech of one of the characters: 'I turned to the sea')
- imagery: the way in which the author uses word pictures
- symbolism

> ### Grade *booster*
>
> If you write about style in the exam, and do it well, you will show the examiner that your grasp of the novel is sophisticated.

> ### Grade *booster*
>
> Your job as a literary critic — because that is what you are when you write your exam essay — is to identify the choices Golding has made and to assess how effective they are.

Setting and atmosphere

It is important to remember that Golding said he set out to write a realistic version of *The Coral Island*. This means that the setting has to be a deserted island. Golding has followed some of the conventions of the original novel by R. M. Ballantyne in giving the boys food and water and in making

Pause for thought

Golding uses a technique called pathetic fallacy, where the weather reflects the mood of the scene:

> sun gazed down like an angry eye   (p. 60)

> short chill of dawn   (p. 187)

What do these quotations suggest about the atmosphere of each scene, and how does this reflect the events at each moment in the novel?

sure they cannot get off the island. However, one major difference between *Lord of the Flies* and *The Coral Island* is that the boys in Golding's novel never try to leave the island. There is no talk of building a raft or a boat. There is simply the idea of being rescued. This gives the setting of the island an added importance, because the boys must make do with what they have.

The island seems to be a tropical one, as it is always warm and there is plenty of ripe fruit on the trees. Golding at times makes use of the weather. The main example of this is the storm that has been developing and which finally breaks at the time of Simon's death. The boys are affected by the weather and it is probably one of the reasons they get so carried away. You have only to think how uncomfortable you feel on a hot sticky day just before a thunderstorm to realise the impact the build-up to the storm has on the boys.

A tropical island setting

Key quotation

The silence of the forest was more oppressive than the heat.   (p. 49)

Parts of the island are lit by bright sunlight and seem safe. Other parts are dark and mysterious. The forest is particularly frightening at times. This reflects a normal human fear of the unknown. Even near home, walking through a dark forest can be a scary prospect. Only Simon enjoys the seclusion of the forest. Jack explores it in order to hunt but never sets up camp there.

The boys inhabit two main parts of the island:
- the edge of the beach near the bathing pool: Ralph and his followers end up here
- Castle Rock: Jack instinctively retreats into a fortress even though there is nothing on the island to harm him

The island is an unusual shape: 'It was roughly boat-shaped: humped near this end with behind them the jumbled descent to the shore' (Chapter 1, p. 26). Jack's castle is described as being almost detached from the rest of the island: 'There, where the island petered out in water, was another island; a rock, almost detached, standing like a fort, facing them across the green with one bold, pink bastion' (p. 26). Creating the island in this way allows Golding to develop the storyline of Jack taking his tribe off to Castle Rock. Making the island boat-shaped is perhaps a joke reference to *The Coral Island*, in which boats play a major role. It is also possible that Golding intended the shape to be symbolic, suggesting that the island itself contains the means of rescue or salvation — in a moral sense.

The contrasts between the safety of the beach, the menace of the forest and mountain, and the security of the castle give the writer scope to move the boys around the island to suit the purposes of the story.

The boys have been presented with a perfect island — their own Garden of Eden. Parallels with the story of the fall of Adam from God's favour in the book of Genesis in the Bible are valid here. The boys fear a mysterious beast that drives them to terrible deeds; in the book of Genesis, the beast that causes the trouble is the serpent. The paradise with which the boys have been presented turns into a nightmare landscape for Ralph as he tries to run and hide from Jack. You could make the point that this represents a view of the way in which humankind has treated the planet.

The pig's head on the stick is clearly an important image — it gives the novel its title, *Lord of the Flies*. This title is also a reference to Beelzebub — one of Satan's henchmen. The image of a head being eaten by flies is disturbing anyway, but becomes even stronger when linked to the devil. The voice Simon hears seems to come from this head. Golding may be asking the reader to think about the role of evil in the boys' lives.

Dialogue

Golding has carefully given the boys the manner of speech that he would have heard in any boys' school at the time the novel was written. The voices are not upper class, though they will sound strange to many school pupils today. Examples of boys' talk are:
- 'my auntie' (Piggy, p. 3)

- 'Daddy taught me.' (Ralph, p. 8)
- 'Take off your togs.' (Jack, p. 20)
- 'waxy', meaning very angry (several boys use this word)
- 'wacco' and 'wizard' (Ralph and Jack at Simon's suggestion of a map)

The speech patterns of the boys are in keeping with Golding's idea of creating a realistic version of *The Coral Island* and come from his own experience of having taught boys like those in the novel.

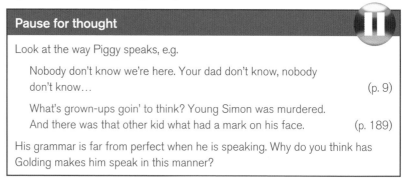

Pause for thought

Look at the way Piggy speaks, e.g.

> Nobody don't know we're here. Your dad don't know, nobody
> don't know… (p. 9)

> What's grown-ups goin' to think? Young Simon was murdered.
> And there was that other kid what had a mark on his face. (p. 189)

His grammar is far from perfect when he is speaking. Why do you think has Golding makes him speak in this manner?

Even though Jack's behaviour becomes more and more savage, his manner of speech does not really alter. This makes his actions seem even more terrible, as they are being carried out by a boy (a choirboy at that) who speaks well and sounds like a young English gentleman.

Two of the words used throughout the novel give the reader a clear indication that the boys are not very mature. The words are 'chief' and 'tribe'. The boys would probably have heard these words used in history lessons or would associate them with cowboy-and-Indian films or adventure stories. When Jack turns into a chief, he is copying a child's idea of what a tribal chief would be like.

Text **focus**

Look closely at the following passage from Ralph's speech to the assembly in Chapter 5 (p. 87):

> And another thing. We nearly set the whole island on fire. And we waste time, rolling rocks, and making little cooking fires. Now I say this and make it a rule, because I'm chief. We won't have a fire anywhere but on the mountain. Ever.

It could be argued that this speech register sounds quite childish. Look at:

- the use of 'and': this is the way that young children construct speech
- the fact that Ralph has to stress that he is chief: again, this is quite a childish thing to do and shows he is insecure
- the use of the word 'ever' to finish off: this is typical of a young child's way of finishing off a point

Note that you do not have to accept this interpretation of the speech. How could you argue that in fact his register shows Ralph as a strong leader?

Description

Places

The island is described in some detail in Chapter 1. As the boys explore their new surroundings the reader gets to see the island. Golding stresses the lush nature of the vegetation.

Note that from this simple opening observation the darkness becomes increasingly important.

The island is a fertile place, with fruit, birds and pigs, so there should be plenty of food. Other features that play a role in the story are:

Key quotation

The shore was fledged with palm trees...The ground beneath them was a bank covered with coarse grass...Behind this was the darkness of the forest proper...

(p. 4)

- the 'great platform of pink granite' that forms the diving board and a natural meeting place
- the lagoon that surrounds the island: this keeps the sea from the island and makes the boys even more cut off while also giving them somewhere to swim (in the bathing pool) and play
- the mountain: this is important because it is the obvious place to light a signal fire and it is also the place where the dead airman lands
- the Castle Rock: this becomes Jack's fortress and it is where Piggy dies

The landscape is always seen through a haze of heat and the temperature never really drops. This removes the problem of the boys having to find clothing or shelter. It also allows Golding to explore the effects of a strange new environment on the boys. The clothes they arrived in are useless on the island and are soon torn on branches or simply thrown away.

Text focus

Read the descriptions of the island in Chapter 1. Golding stresses the clean, pure aspects of the landscape. The water is 'peacock' blue. Imagine the effect if the water around the island were described as 'muddy brown'.

Make a list of the descriptions from Chapter 1, then do the same for descriptions of the island from the final chapter. Look at how the pleasant and lush landscape has changed by the end of the novel.

People

There are clear descriptions of some of the main characters. This helps the reader to picture them. It is important that Jack and Ralph are the two biggest boys physically. Ralph is described as having the build that suggests he might develop into a boxer, although 'there was a mildness about his mouth and eyes that proclaimed no devil' (p. 5). This tells the reader that although Ralph is strong he is likely to be gentle.

Key quotation

Jack is described as:

tall, thin, and bony: and his hair was red beneath the black cap. His face was crumpled and freckled, and ugly without silliness. Out of this face stared two light blue eyes, frustrated now, and turning, or ready to turn, to anger.

(p. 16)

Pause for thought

Golding does not give clear descriptions of the younger boys. This seems to reflect the attitude of Ralph and Jack towards them: they group them together as the 'littluns' and pay them relatively little attention. Why do you think Golding does not give us a clearer idea of the younger boys as individuals?

Key quotation

...mildness about his mouth and eyes that proclaimed no devil.

(p. 5)

The contrast between the descriptions of Ralph and Jack is very strong and deliberately links physical appearance with character. From the first time we see each boy we are aware that Ralph will tend to be mild in nature while Jack can become angry very quickly.

This of course turns out to be true. Piggy is not described very clearly at all. He is simply a fat boy who is short-sighted and has asthma. The lack of description of Piggy reflects the fact that the boys might not have noticed much else about him. Golding encourages us to see Piggy as the others do. Roger is a dark-haired boy who has a dark and sinister look about him.

Viewpoint

The viewpoint of the novel is the position from which the author tells the story. For example, Golding could have chosen to tell it in the first person, perhaps through the eyes of Ralph or Jack. This would have created a very different novel, as we would have had a one-sided view of events and of the characters.

Grade booster

Recognising the technique of writing in the third person and including it in your essay (if appropriate to the essay title) is a high-level skill.

Instead, the novel is written in the third person. This means it is written using 'he/him' rather than 'I/me'. It allows the author to act as narrator (storyteller). Golding does not interfere in the narrative as some narrators do. He does not deliberately mislead the reader. For example, we know that the beast is nothing other than a dead airman. This technique puts the reader ahead of the characters and creates dramatic tension.

Golding does not use the technique of telling us what the different boys are thinking. The characters' own words reveal their thoughts and states of mind. The fact that Jack shouts 'Choir! Stand still!' tells us a great deal about him and the position he holds in the eyes of the choirboys.

Simon's confusion at the time of his hallucinations in front of the pig's head comes through from the confused conversation that he thinks he is having with the 'Lord of the Flies'. We do not need to be told that he is confused. It is clear from the fact that the Lord of the Flies speaks to Simon that he is in a disturbed state of mind. He imagines the pig's head speaking in the voice of a disapproving authority figure. However, note that 'waxy' is a schoolboy word, not one that a teacher would really use, showing that Simon's image of authority is itself a little childish and confused.

Key quotation

'I'm warning you. I'm going to get waxy. D'you see?'

(p. 158)

Pause for thought

The presentation of Simon's fit comes to us through his own confused eyes. We experience the strange visions and odd conversation along with Simon. How effective do you feel this is? How else could Simon's feelings have been portrayed at this point?

Text **focus**

For much of the time Golding is simply the invisible storyteller, describing events to us in the third person. However, a characteristic technique that he uses at times is to tell the story from the viewpoint of one character while still writing in the third person.

Read the passage in Chapter 12 from 'Most, he was beginning to dread the curtain that might waver in his brain' to 'Hide, then' (pp. 218–19). This passage takes us into Ralph's thought patterns as he flees from Jack and the hunters. The image of 'a deep grumbling noise, as though the forest itself were angry with him' suggests Ralph's sense of being under threat. In addition, we share Ralph's experience in that we are not yet told that the noise comes from the fire. The 'ululations were scribbled excruciatingly as on slate' suggest the classroom experience of chalk on a board, as well as Ralph's anguish.

In the three lines that follow this, Golding attempts to convey Ralph's desperate efforts to think fast:

Break the line.

A tree.

Hide, and let them pass.

How would this be different if Golding described the events in the normal way? For example: 'Ralph tried to think fast. He considered breaking through the line of hunters, or climbing a tree…'.

Watch out for other occasions where Golding uses this technique. It tends to correspond to the most dramatic parts of the story.

Imagery

The term 'imagery' refers to the kinds of word pictures an author creates to help us imagine what is being described. There are two kinds of imagery an author can use:

- **simile:** when one thing is compared with another, using 'like' or 'as'
- **metaphor:** when something is described as if it actually is something else

Golding uses this kind of imagery throughout the novel. The images the reader has of the island and of the boys come from direct description. The language does sometimes become more poetic, for example in Chapter 1:

Key quotation

The coral was scribbled in the sea as though a giant had bent down to reproduce the shape of the island in a flowing, chalk line but tired before he had finished.

(p. 26)

Even such images are linked to the way a child might see things. The act of tracing around an object but getting bored before the end is something a child might do.

The following quotation describes how Ralph's thought process was so complicated that it was a maze of ideas.

He lost himself in a maze of thoughts... (p. 81)

Pause for thought

Look at these other examples of imagery. Identify whether the quotation is a simile or a metaphor and then write a few lines explaining the effect of the language used.

1 'the folds were stiff like cardboard' (p. 82)

2 'Now he saw the landman's view of the swell and it seemed like the breathing of some stupendous creature…the sleeping leviathan breathed out…' (pp. 114–15)

3 'these flies found Simon…They tickled under his nostrils and played leapfrog on his thighs' (p. 152)

4 'Simon was inside the mouth.' (p. 159)

5 'Nothing prospered but the flies who blackened their lord and made the spilt guts look like a heap of glistening coal.' (p. 160)

6 'The light was unearthly. The Lord of the Flies hung on his stick like a black ball.' (p. 160)

Grade *booster*

If in the exam you find you are not sure whether an image is a simile or a metaphor, just call it an image. The important thing is to show how it is used rather than to identify it using the correct technical term.

Golding does not write in a flowery, poetic style. He is concerned with getting across the thoughts and actions of the boys and there are no lengthy passages of writing that are not directly connected with the story.

The description of the dead airman at the start of Chapter 6 is very matter of fact. Even though Sam and Eric find the dead man terrifying, the reader knows what the 'beast' really is. This allows us to observe how the boys respond to the news of the beast without having to work out what it actually is. Golding's choice of technique means that the reader's attention is focused on the boys and not on whether there really is a dangerous monster on the island.

Symbolism

When an author uses an image, something is compared with something else. Symbolism is related to imagery, but it is not nearly so obvious. A symbol is something that the author uses consistently to represent or 'stand for' something else. There is also rather more room for personal interpretation here: not all critics interpret a symbol in exactly the same way.

The whole of *Lord of the Flies* is symbolic. Golding uses the closed world of the island to represent the world outside. Each boy represents a type of person. The kinds of behaviour we see reflect the behaviour of groups of people in the wider world. There are characters in the novel and groups of people in life who:

- take delight in hurting the weak
- try to lead by example
- are good thinkers but are not physically strong
- are physically strong but have few ideas

Golding uses the island as a symbol of the planet on which we all live. It was almost perfect to start with but becomes dangerous and damaged through the actions of humans.

The boys use the conch as a symbol of power. It gives the holder the right to speak without interruption — at least at the start of the novel. Piggy has an idea of how a sound is made using the shell and this ancient form of trumpet comes to symbolise law and order. It is significant that Piggy is holding the conch when Roger sends the rock down on him: the last trace of order is smashed along with Piggy himself.

Ralph blows the conch

Alamy/Pictorial Press Ltd

> **Pause for thought**
>
> It is interesting to chart the movement and status of Piggy's glasses throughout the novel. Does their deterioration mirror that of the boys?

Piggy's glasses are useful in a practical way because they are used to light the fire. They also symbolise wisdom. When Jack steals them he gains the ability to light the fire but none of Piggy's cleverness. The glasses also represent a link to the old world of school and the adult way of doing things.

Golding's use of light and darkness

During the day the island is bathed in light: 'The sand, trembling beneath the heat-haze' (Chapter 1, p. 14) and 'They faced each other on the bright beach' (Chapter 3, p. 55). In reality fair-skinned children would probably suffer badly from the intense sunlight. This is not the case in the novel: daytime is a time of safety, at least at the start of the novel.

The boys are happy during the day, but: 'When the sun sank, darkness dropped on the island like an extinguisher and soon the shelters were full of restlessness' (Chapter 4, p. 61). Fear of the dark is a natural human emotion. The boys are affected strongly by it but this is not unusual for children. How many small children like to have a light on while they fall asleep? It is significant, however, that the older children refuse to give in to their fears at first. Ralph focuses on the fire as their source of rescue, during the early chapters. Nevertheless, Jack's tribe becomes increasingly desperate to keep its fire alight. On the other side of the island, in Chapter 10, Piggy finally admits 'the double function of the fire…to be a hearth now and a comfort until they slept' (p. 179).

> ## *Text* focus
>
> The fire is important throughout the novel. What do the following quotations show you about the role of fire in the novel?
>
> > This was the first time he had admitted the double function of the fire. Certainly one was to send up a beckoning column of smoke; but the other was to be a hearth now and a comfort until they slept.
> >
> > (p. 179)
>
> > There was something good about a fire. Something overwhelmingly good.
> >
> > (p. 180)
>
> > The flames, as though they were a kind of wild life, crept as a jaguar creeps on its belly towards a line of birch-like saplings…
> >
> > (p. 44)
>
> > …the fire racing forward like a tide.
> >
> > (p. 222)

Symbolic events

The fire at the beginning not only foreshadows the larger fire at the end but is also symbolic of the chaos that descends when civilised behaviour gives way to the savage within.

The pitting of huts against hunting is symbolic of the conflicting forces of civilisation versus savagery. The irony is that both are necessary for survival as we need both food and shelter.

Simon's death (juxtaposed with the floating out to sea of the dead airman) and Piggy's death are both markers in the descent into savagery. Other markers are the destruction and theft of the glasses: initially just one lens is broken, showing that they are losing their civilised nature, then, when the glasses are taken, Piggy loses his sight completely, symbolising the end of clear-sightedness and the descent into instinct and savagery.

The events surrounding the conch are also symbolic because the conch is a symbol of order at the start of the novel, but by the end of Chapter 11 it is destroyed completely, showing the total breakdown of civilised behaviour on the island.

Review your learning

(Answers are given on p. 93.)

1. Why do you think Golding chose this setting for the novel?
2. How are night and day used symbolically in the novel?
3. What is the symbolic significance of the conch?
4. What is the symbolic significance of the fire?

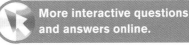

More interactive questions and answers online.

Tackling the exam

- **What is an essay?**
- **How should you plan your answer?**
- **How can you use PEE effectively?**
- **How can you follow an argument through a whole essay?**
- **How might mind maps help?**
- **What are the differences between higher and foundation tiers?**

Essay writing: hints and tips

A typical essay will usually contain:
- an introduction, where you suggest what you are going to say
- the main body of the essay, where you make points backed up with evidence
- a conclusion, where you sum up what you have said

A typical essay on prose will contain comments on many aspects of the work. You will have to decide what is required on the basis of the individual question, but you should be prepared to write about:
- plot (related to the question)
- character
- setting
- dialogue
- language
- purpose
- effectiveness
- mood
- point of view
- context

You will also need to give good support for comments you make.

Planning your answer

It is very important that you plan your answer before you begin writing it in an examination. Examiners will see that you have thought about what you are going to say and, although this will not get you any extra marks, it will show that you have thought carefully about what you are writing and will make a good impression.

To help you with your planning it is important to have prepared yourself thoroughly for the examination.

Knowing your way around the text

No matter how good you are at writing essays, there is no substitute for knowing the text well. You are able to take the book into the exam with you if you are following the AQA or OCR specifications, but it must not contain your notes. (You are not allowed to take the text into the exam for the WJEC or CCEA specifications.) This means you could end up spending a long time trying to find an incident or a particular quotation unless you know where things come in the text.

A useful exercise is:

1 Write down in a notebook the key events of the novel.
2 Write a one-paragraph description of each of the major characters.
3 Write a brief summary of what the writer set out to do.

The time you have for writing is quite short, so you need to spend as little of it as possible looking up quotations and reminding yourself of the text.

Although you will get no marks for simply retelling the story, it is important to know it very well. You should have a sound grasp of the following:

- the main events
- the sequence in which they occur
- the part played by each character in them

It is also helpful, though not essential, to be able to refer confidently to the chapters or sections. This is relatively easy for *Lord of the Flies*, as each chapter has a title that summarises the action.

The question

Breaking down the question

If you feel under pressure in the exam, it is tempting to read the question quickly and start writing a response immediately. Stop! You should read the question carefully, at least twice, and attempt to break it down into parts to work out exactly what you are being asked to do. This will help to make sure that you answer the question that is being asked and not the one that you think is being asked or for which you have prepared. A useful technique is to underline the key words. You should practise under-lining or highlighting the key words in every new question you meet.

Below is a higher-tier question (with key words in bold). It is an example of the sort of question that may appear on the WJEC specification:

What do **you think of 'the beast'** in the novel and the **way it is presented** in *Lord of the Flies*?

You could break this down in the following way:

1 How does the idea of the beast emerge? What is there in human nature that makes people afraid of the unknown?
2 How does Golding use dramatic timing to show how the beast becomes more and more important? If Sam and Eric had found the dead airman earlier or had stayed longer to find out what was on the mountain how would this have affected the fear of the beast?
3 What you think about how Jack exploits the fear of the beast in order to make his own position more powerful?
4 What you think about why Simon's ideas about the beast make him seem even stranger to the others, and how his interest in the beast leads to his death?
5 What do you think the beast is, and what do you think Golding is trying to say by using the beast as an important symbol in the novel?

Interpreting the question

Grade *booster*

If the meaning of a question seems unclear or open to interpretation, consider choosing another question — if there is a choice. If you still decide to tackle this question, the important thing is to make your interpretation clear.

Sometimes the question is open to more than one interpretation. For the question above you can look at the beast as:

- the fear of a real monster on the island
- something inside everyone that makes us afraid
- a dark force that lets some people take advantage of the fear of others
- a devil-like character that causes the boys to behave in ways they would not do otherwise

You would be unwise to try to consider all these options at great length in your essay, so you would need to identify three or four main points you thought you could write about well, and make these clear in your opening paragraph.

The form of your plan

You may find it helpful to use a diagram of some sort — perhaps a spider diagram or flow chart. This may help you to keep your mind open to new ideas as you plan, so that you can slot them in. You could make a list instead, but this is more difficult to add to.

You will probably need to get the important points down on paper in some form before you arrange them. If you have drawn a spider diagram, arranging them is a simple matter of numbering the branches in the best possible order.

Referring to the author and title

You can refer to Golding either by name (spell it correctly) or as 'the author'. You should never use his first name (William) — this sounds as if you know him personally. You can also save time by giving the title in full the first time you refer to it, with 'Flies' in brackets after it, and then using the one-word title after that.

Writing in an appropriate style

Remember that you are expected to write in an *appropriate* way for a formal exam essay. Examiners' reports every year give a range of inappropriate language used by candidates. These instances can make amusing reading, but they have lost the candidates marks. To use a technical term, you must write in a suitable register. This means:

- *not* using colloquial language or slang (except when quoting dialogue): 'Jack's a nasty piece of work. A bit of a toe-rag really.'
- *not* becoming too personal: 'Ralph is like my mate, right, 'cos he...'
- using suitable phrases for an academic essay, for example 'It could be argued that', not 'I reckon that...'

The first person ('I')

At one time it was thought to be a bad thing to write in the first person (using 'I'), but now this is acceptable as long as you do not do it all the way through the essay. You could use it to your advantage, especially in the opening and closing paragraphs, where you state your views and then give your considered opinion.

Occasional use of 'I feel' or 'I think' is fine. You should have a group of phrases that you know you can use, and vary them so that your answer does not sound the same all the way through. Examples might include:

- some people feel that
- it could be said that
- in my opinion
- another argument is
- a major factor in this is
- to sum up, I would say

Remember: you are out to make a good impression on an examiner who has never met you.

Grade **booster**

Although your own English is not, strictly, being marked when you write a literature essay, better candidates demonstrate their grasp of the novel through the way in which they write.

At this point you should think of the different comparing words that you have in your vocabulary. Add ten more of your own to the list below. They can be phrases or single words:

- whereas
- however
- although
- on the other hand
- alternatively

Above all, remember that *essay writing is a skill and requires practice*.

Using PEE effectively

PEE (**P**oint, **E**vidence, **E**xplanation) is an important essay-writing technique that will enable you to write effectively in the examination.

You need to make your initial point and back this up with a quotation from the passage before explaining your idea further. For example, an answer to the question: 'What do you consider to be the importance of Piggy in *Lord of the Flies*, and how does Golding present him?' may include the following:

1 Point made about Piggy's importance, related to the conch

2 Quotation illustrates point

3 Explanation of the quotation

4 Further development of idea related to the conch with the use of the embedded quotation 'asthma' to clarify the point

Piggy is a very important character in **Lord of the Flies**. He is with Ralph when he finds the conch. Ralph does not know it is a conch, just a shell, but Piggy does and he knows how to use it to call the other boys as he tells Ralph about seeing someone use a similar conch at home:**1** 'A conch he called it. He used to blow it and then his mum would come. It's ever so valuable…'**2**

Piggy shows great knowledge throughout the novel. Here he uses his knowledge to tell Ralph what the shell is and what it can do. Without Piggy's knowledge Ralph would not have known that you can blow into it and this can be used to help call the others together for a meeting.**3** It is the conch that gives Ralph the authority when he calls this meeting and allows him to be voted Chief. The conch also highlight's Piggy's weaknesses. Although he knows how it can be blown to create a sound he can't do it himself because of his 'asthma'.**4**

This is part of a good answer and with further development should gain a high mark.

Grade *booster* !

It is important to make the individual quotations you select brief and your explanations detailed. This can help you develop more ideas and points into your answers.

Foundation and higher tiers

You will be entered for the exam at either the foundation or the higher tier.

Foundation tier

The foundation-tier questions are easier than those for the higher tier, but the highest grade you can get is a C. The skills you need for either tier are the same, but if you know you are being entered for the foundation tier, be especially careful not to do any of the things listed under the heading 'What you will not get marks for' on p. 74.

The foundation-tier questions may be based on character rather than themes or style. They generally involve a number of bullet-point hints to help you answer. Make sure you think about these hints and make use of them. You will probably find it helpful to use them as the basis of your essay plan.

AQA- or CCEA-style question

What do you think of Ralph's leadership skills?
Include in your answer:
- What does Ralph do?
- What ideas does he have as a leader and what do you think of these ideas?
- How does Golding show Ralph's leadership qualities?

Plan of action

When answering a foundation-tier question, you will be given some bullet points to guide you. Use these to help you plan your answer.

His ideas/what he does:
- fire
- shelters
- rescue
- democratic style
- use of the conch for order
- the importance of the rules

You will need to pick out examples of at least three of these ideas and discuss them, making sure you comment on what you think about these ideas and Ralph's leadership style.

The methods Golding uses to show what Ralph is like as a leader.
- symbolism
- what he looks like
- how he acts
- comparisons with Jack

All this will be too much for the exam, so you need to pick some of them to discuss in more detail.

OCR-style question

Explore the use of the conch in the novel during any **ONE** or **TWO** moments.
Back up your comments with references to the novel.

Plan of action

Include some of the following areas:

- What is the conch used for?
- How does it change during the novel?
- What does it represent?
- Two or three key incidents involving the conch.

WJEC-style question

'Golding has experience of teaching boys, so he knows what they are like. This is clearly shown in *Lord of the Flies*.'
Do you agree with this statement?

Refer to some moments in the novel to argue for or against this statement. Explain your ideas.

Plan of action

Remember that context is assessed by the WJEC board, so those students using this specification will need to comment on context throughout their answer. Questions like this one will help you do this as you will need to write about:

- Golding's background as a teacher
- When the novel was written and when it was set — how boys behaved then and how this comes across in the novel

The question asks you to select specific moments in the novel to write about. You may wish to look at:

The arrival of Jack and his choir and how they act at this point

- one of the meetings
- hunting
- bullying of Piggy
- the hierarchy of the boys
- the boys' attitude to adults
- their childishness

Grade *booster*

The WJEC mark scheme states that, in order to gain a mark in the top band for this paper, your answer must be detailed and make relevant reference to the text to support your judgements.

Higher tier

At higher tier you may not be given bullet-point hints to help you. If you are, think about them and consider using them as the basis of your essay plan. If you are not given any bullet-point hints, you should write them yourself in your essay plan, so you need to think carefully about what the question is asking you to do. There may be several elements to the question — this is discussed in the section on 'Breaking down the question' on p. 63.

Below are some examples of higher-tier type questions.

AQA-, OCR- or CCEA-style question

What are Golding's thoughts about leaders and leadership and how does he express these in *Lord of the Flies*?

You will need to brainstorm your ideas first, before attempting an answer. This is really important because, if you do not plan your answer, it may be disorganised, you may run out of things to say and you may miss out some crucial points.

For this question you may think about:

- Who are the leaders in the novel?
- Who are not leaders and why aren't they?
- What is Golding trying to say about leadership?
- Look in more detail at Ralph and Jack

Ralph: democratic

- Why is he chosen as the leader?
- What does he offer as a leader? (Think about how important the conch, the fire, shelters and rescue are to him)
- The link to Piggy and his intelligence
- He thinks rationally, rather than acts in a violent manner
- Golding's purpose — why does Ralph's leadership fail?
- Is there any hope for his leadership style?

Jack: dictator

- Why do the others do what he says?
- The importance of Roger to him
- Beating of Wilfred
- Uses the other boys' fear to his advantage
- His fearsome appearance and angry nature
- Hunting and face paint
- The importance of action/violence and hunting
- He acts on instinct rather than thinking things through rationally
- Golding's purpose — what he is saying about Jack's style

Within your answer you will not have time to deal with all these areas, but they can be used as a guide to decide which points you may wish to write about.

WJEC-style question

'Golding has experience of teaching boys, so he knows what they are like. This is clearly shown in *Lord of the Flies*.'
Do you agree with this statement? Refer in detail to the text in your answer.

Plan of action

See the plan for the foundation-tier question.

In addition to this you might consider:

- If he shows evidence of not knowing what the boys are like, e.g. is Roger too evil/unrealistic?
- Do boys follow leaders like Jack?
- Would Jack's style of leadership really work?
- Are the characters too stereotyped?

Review your learning

(Answers are given on p. 94.)

1. What is an essay?
2. Why is it important to plan your answer?
3. How do you use PEE effectively?

More interactive questions and answers online.

Assessment Objectives and skills

- **What are the Assessment Objectives?**
- **How do the Assessment Objectives apply to different exam boards?**
- **How will your essay be marked?**
- **What skills are you required to show?**
- **How can you gain extra marks related to each Assessment Objective?**
- **How can you improve your grade?**
- **What is needed for an A*?**

Assessment Objectives (AOs)

The Assessment Objectives that you will be assessed on are:

AO1

Respond to texts critically and imaginatively; select and evaluate relevant textual detail to illustrate and support interpretations.

AO2

Explain how language, structure and form contribute to writers' presentation of ideas, themes and settings.

AO4

Relate texts to their social, cultural and historical contexts; explain how texts have been influential and significant to self and other readers in different contexts and at different times.

How AOs apply to the different exam boards

- AQA assesses AO1 and AO2.
- OCR assesses AO1 and AO2.

Grade **booster**

Whatever the board,
you are likely to impress
the examiner if you
show some awareness
of the 'social, cultural
and historical contexts'
that have influenced
the novel.

- WJEC assesses AO1, AO2 and AO4.
- CCEA assesses AO1 and AO2.

How will your essay be marked?

An examiner marking your exam essay will be trying to give you marks, but will be able to do so only if you succeed in fulfilling the key Assessment Objectives for English literature.

What skills do you need to show?

Let's break the Assessment Objectives down to see what they mean.

AO1

- **Respond to texts critically:** this means you must say what you think of the novel and why. You are being asked to **evaluate** it. This involves realising that the author has made choices, and giving your views on how effective these choices are.
- **imaginatively:** this means your ideas need to be interesting and exploratory. You will need to see themes, ideas and settings in an imaginative manner, coming up with answers that explore the text and the potential meanings, and producing more than one interpretation of an idea or moment.
- **select...relevant textual detail to illustrate and support interpretations:** this means giving short quotations from the text, or referring to details in the text, to support your views.
- **evaluate** means commenting on the textual detail you have selected, relating your comments to the question that has been set. The best candidates are able to see the events of parts of the novel and relate them to what Golding was trying to say as a whole.

AO2

Explain how **language**, **structure** and **form** contribute to writers' presentation of **ideas**, **themes** and **settings**.

- **'language, structure and form':** the word '**language**' refers to Golding's use of words. Look at the first description of Ralph. The author chooses to focus on parts of his face that make him look kind and calm. There are many other ways in which Golding could have made the point that Ralph is not naturally violent. He could simply have stated it. Instead the reader has to do a little detective work.

The word '**structure**' refers to the overall shape of the novel, as discussed in the *Plot and structure* section of this guide. Remember, for example, that the novel begins and ends with a military conflict raging around the boys. They are transported into their own world by war and it is a warship that rescues them.

The word '**form**' is more vague. In the case of *Lord of the Flies*, the form is determined partly by Golding's wish to write a realistic version of *The Coral Island*. The novel is divided up into twelve chapters. Each chapter title makes it clear what the chapter will be about. This form helps to show the gradual descent of the boys from civilisation to savagery in a clear, organised manner.

Other devices that link to form and structure are Ralph's flashbacks to home life and sections of the novel where two events are happening at the same time (Simon's experience with the Lord of the Flies in Chapter 8 is happening at the same time as Jack is setting up his own 'tribe').

- **writers' presentation of ideas, themes and settings:** the word '**ideas**' refers to what Golding is writing about and trying to say in the novel. There are many things that Golding is trying to say in *Lord of the Flies*, which are discussed throughout this guide.

For example, if you were writing about the fire and how it is presented in the novel, you would need to think about what point about fire is being made by Golding on several levels:

- It is dangerous
- It creates warmth and comfort
- It can be used for cooking
- It generates smoke to create a signal for them to be rescued

It can also be related to the destructive nature of the boys and humankind, as they are prepared to destroy where they live because of a disagreement, just as at this time there was the great threat of a nuclear war. This can be linked to the idea of the island being a microcosm of the world.

The word '**themes**' refers to a group of ideas that the author explores. You can read much more about the themes of this novel on pp. 43–50. You need to be able to write about the themes of the novel in relation to the question you have chosen to answer.

The word '**settings**' refers to the various locations in which the events of the novel take place. This is dealt with in more detail on pp. 51–53.

AO4

Context

If you are trying to display knowledge of this area, do not treat the English literature exam as though it were history. For example, knowing that *Lord of the Flies* was written during the Cold War might help your understanding

> **Grade *booster***
>
> By developing these points in detail you are showing the evaluative, insightful and exploratory skills required for an A* grade.

of themes, but you should not get side-tracked and start to write at length about post-war Europe. Your task is to write about the novel.

The AO in the mark scheme specifically says:

> Relate texts to their social, cultural and historical contexts; explain how texts have been influential and significant to self and other readers in different contexts and at different times.

- **Relate texts to their social, cultural and historical contexts:** this means you have to show some understanding of the context in which Golding wrote the novel. So you have to understand, for example, that British schoolboys in the 1950s were genuinely taught to live by the same values that the boys in the novel start out with — decency, fair play and a sense that being British was very important because it meant that you were superior.

- **explain how texts have been influential and significant to self and other readers in different contexts and at different times:** this requires an awareness that there have been different interpretations of texts at different times. For instance, readers in the 1950s will have seen the novel very differently from a reader today, as many of them will have had some direct contact with the Second World War and will be able to relate directly to some of the events in the novel.

The word '**influential**' means how a text or idea within a text can influence a reader's thoughts and ideas about something, both when the novel was written and now. This could be linked to ideas in the novel on leadership. When the novel was written there were different leaders in power across the world and, as a result, different threats to humankind.

The word '**significant**' means how individual readers can relate to a character, idea or text and see something they recognise of themselves or their society from a character or situation in a text.

What you will not get marks for

The Assessment Objectives tell you what you *will* get marks for. It is also important to know what you *will not* get marks for:

- **Retelling the story.** You can be sure that the examiner marking your essay knows the story inside out. He or she may be a teacher who has taught the novel, and will not want to be told the story again. The examiner follows a mark scheme and will probably be referring to 'grade descriptors' giving pointers to the features to be expected from essays at each of the grades. A key feature of the lowest grades is 'retelling the story'. Don't do it.

- **Quoting long passages.** You will waste time and gain no marks by quoting long passages from the novel. Use your judgement, but it will probably never be necessary for you to quote more than two sentences at a time.
- **Identifying figures of speech or other features.** You will never gain marks simply for identifying figures of speech, such as similes or metaphors. Similarly, you will gain no marks for pointing out that 'Golding uses a lot of verbs in this passage'. You will gain marks only by identifying these features and saying why the author has used them and how effective you think they are.
- **Giving unsubstantiated opinions.** The examiner will be keen to give you marks for your opinions but only if they are supported by reasoned argument and references to the text. Hence you will get no marks for writing: 'Everyone thinks that Piggy is completely useless but I don't.' But you will get marks for: 'Although some of the boys call Piggy "useless" it is clear that he is actually responsible for many of the ideas that make life bearable on the island.'

Improving your grade

Most students can immediately make some improvement in grade by recognising what it is that they are being asked to do. All written tasks can be broken down into these simple areas:

- What did the writer set out to do?
- How did the writer go about doing it?
- Was the writer successful?

Many students concentrate on the second point and neglect the others. This results in a lengthy retelling of the story. There is nothing wrong with referring to the story enough to make your point, but if all you do in your essay is retell the story you have carried out only a fairly basic task. The plot of most great novels could be given to a class of eight-year-olds, who would then retell the story and draw a lovely picture. Remember: simply retelling the story is not a high-level skill.

You should consider the first point before you begin to write any lengthy answer. You must try to grasp what the writer set out to do. In other words, was Golding writing a story for his own amusement or did he have a higher purpose in mind?

When you come to discuss the way in which the writer went about achieving his aims, you need to:

- decide what it is you want to say
- select the parts of the text that support what you want to say

Ladder of skills

It is useful at this stage to look at the criteria that will be used to assess your written work. You can think of the following levels of skill as a ladder guiding you from basic skills to more advanced ones.

Grade F candidates

- make an involved personal response to the effects of language, structure and form in texts
- show some awareness of key ideas, themes or arguments
- support views by reference to significant features or details
- make some straightforward connections and comparisons between texts, suggesting how this contributes to readers' enjoyment
- are aware that some aspects of texts relate to their specific social, cultural and historical contexts

Grade C candidates

- understand and demonstrate how writers use ideas, themes and settings in texts to affect the reader
- respond personally to the effects of language, structure and form
- refer to textual details to support their views and reactions
- explain the relevance and impact of connections and comparisons between texts
- show awareness of some of the social, cultural and historical contexts of texts and of how these influence their meanings for contemporary and modern readers
- convey ideas clearly and appropriately

Grade A candidates

- respond enthusiastically and critically to texts, showing imagination and originality in developing alternative approaches and interpretations
- confidently explore and evaluate how language, structure and form contribute to writers' varied ways of presenting ideas, themes and settings and how they achieve specific effects on readers
- make illuminating connections and comparisons between texts
- identify and comment on the impact of the social, cultural and historical contexts of texts on different readers and times
- convey ideas persuasively and cogently, supporting them with apt textual reference

Getting an A*

To reach the highest level you need to consider whether the writer has been successful. If you think Golding set out to examine human nature and the ways people react to difficult situations, do you think he was successful?

A higher-level answer will always contain the personal response of the student. Do not be afraid to say 'I feel that…' or 'I believe…'. You must of course have some evidence for what you suggest.

You need to be able consistently to be insightful and exploratory when it comes to both the text and the task. In other words you must be answering the question in a manner that shows your thoughts are original, closely related to the text and are exploring in close detail what the writer was doing.

You will need to use frequent quotations, which will be embedded into your answer. This means that your quotations will often be short (no more than a few words) and these will add support to the comments you are making throughout your answer.

For example:

Golding shows that if there is a threat to Jack as leader, it is Roger in his 'only just avoiding pushing' Jack out of the way in his advance upon Samneric to show him the proper way to torture.

To evaluate language, form and structure you must be able not only to discuss the effect of various techniques used in the novel but also to discuss the overall effects on the reader and the meaning of the text.

To be imaginative and original means that your ideas need to be your own, relevant and plausible, and not something that is likely to be said by the majority of candidates.

Review your learning

(Answers are given on p. 94.)

1. What does AO1 assess?
2. What does AO2 assess?
3. What does AO4 assess?
4. Which AOs does your exam board require you to focus on?
5. What should you not do in your answers?
6. What is needed to gain an A*?

More interactive questions and answers online.

Sample essays

- Why are structuring and signposting important?
- What are the main principles for using quotations?
- How can you improve a character- or theme-based essay answer?

Structuring your essay

Think in terms of your essay having three sections:

1 beginning (introduction)
2 middle (development)
3 end (conclusion)

You need good ideas to write a good essay, but you also need to demonstrate that you can put them together in a logical order, developing them to reach your conclusion. Here are some hints for each section of the essay.

Beginning (introduction)

Do not spend half your essay time on an introduction and then find you have no time to develop and conclude your essay. This is a common mistake. Instead, limit yourself to an opening paragraph of no more than about 100 words. This should:

- refer to the question and give an initial response to it
- show that you have understood it
- show how you intend to answer it, hinting at the views you will put forward
- explain your own view if there is more than one possible interpretation

You may also need to give some background here. Do so by all means — but briefly.

Beware of starting your essay in a way that forces you to write a list. In answering the question 'Consider the importance of the beast', you should not begin by writing 'The way that the beast is important is…'. If you do this your whole essay will have to be a simple list. It is far better to write: 'The beast comes to be important in several ways. One of these is…'. This structure allows you to develop the essay logically while still keeping the question closely in focus.

Grade **booster**

Do not write things such as 'In this essay I am going to…'. Try to reflect the question but do not simply turn it around.

Example: grade A* answer

> What does Golding think about leaders and leadership in
> *Lord of the Flies* and how does he show this?

In *Lord of the Flies* there are two very distinct leaders: Ralph and Jack.**1** Ralph is a more civilised leader who leads with a 'mildness' and by focusing on what others need the most and operates a democratic system shown by his comment to the other boys: 'Which is better, law and rescue, or hunting and breaking things up?' He sees the importance of law and order throughout the novel.**2**

Jack is a much more dictatorial figure and he tells others that he is the leader and instructs them in what to do. He expects no discussion or argument, telling the others 'I'm going to be chief,' when he forms his breakaway group. He does what he thinks is best for others such as when he says 'we need meat', but he is selfish and does what he wants to do telling the other boys in Chapter 8 'I'm going off by myself. He can catch his own pigs. Anyone who wants to hunt when I do can come too.' Here Golding shows Jack's childish side, but also shows his desire to break Ralph's leadership stronghold, even if in an inexpert manner. If he had asked the boys 'Who wants a powerful hunter like me as chief?' he may have been more successful, but he makes the classic mistake of asking a question in a manner that is unlikely to have the boys challenge Ralph while he is in front of them.**3** By presenting two very different styles of leadership, Golding is showing us that there are different ways of leading, but not all are successful or good.**4**

1 This is a strong opening. The candidate immediately focuses on the terms of the question and clearly states a bold and focused opinion that both leaders are very different.

2 There is now more detail given on Ralph's character in terms of his leadership qualities, but only in terms of an introduction, including an embedded quotation 'mildness' illustrating his calm nature.

3 This is contrasted with Jack's style of leadership. Note the use of quotations to support the ideas and the exploration of Jack's unsuccessful attempt to undermine Ralph's authority.

4 There is also a focus on the writer and his intentions. These paragraphs act as an introduction to the material that follows, which will show why the candidate thinks this way.

Middle (development)

This part of the essay is in some ways easier than the other two. If you have made a good plan, you know what you are doing by now and can follow your plan, point by point, presenting your argument with appropriate evidence to back it up (see the next section, 'Using quotations and referring to the text').

Your biggest challenge in this part of the essay will probably be to make it flow smoothly from point to point, showing the examiner how the points connect. The examiner should never start to read a paragraph and think 'Hang on — how did we get here?'

Pause for thought

Part of the secret to good organisation is to plan properly in the first place, arranging your points in a logical way so that one leads on from the next. However, it is also important to use appropriate link words and phrases. These signpost your ideas, giving the reader an idea of what sort of thing is coming next and how it relates to the previous idea. Look at the words and phrases in the table on p. 80, with the ideas that they contain. It is important not to overuse any of these. Try not to begin any two paragraphs in a row with the same word, and certainly not two sentences in a row. Can you think of any other words you could use?

Word/phrase	Idea it contains
However Yet	An exception is coming: '*However*, Piggy can assert himself if necessary.' Yet can be used without the comma
Despite this Nevertheless Nonetheless	Signal an apparent contradiction: '*Despite this*, Jack admires Ralph's strength.'
On the other hand	Signals a balanced alternative: '*On the other hand*, it could be argued that…' Useful for showing you realise that different interpretations of the text are valid
By contrast	Compares two features. A paragraph on the leadership style of Ralph could be used to contrast sharply with the way that Jack runs his tribe
Similarly	Gives a similar example: '*Similarly*, Ralph realises that Piggy is right.'
Another example	'*Another example* of Golding using schoolboy language to stress how young the characters are comes in…'
In addition	Introduces a point making the previous one even stronger. After a paragraph on how the boys miss the first chance of rescue: '*In addition*, the boys' society is already beginning to break down.'
Above all	Introduces the most important of several points: '*Above all*, the fire is the one real hope of rescue.'

End (conclusion)

The conclusion should draw your arguments to a logical close, but it should not simply repeat them in a different form.

If you have explored two sides of an argument, use the conclusion to state which side you personally take. This is a good time to make a personal comment, for example: 'Having looked at both sides of this question, I feel that…'.

Your conclusion should, above all, refer back to the question, showing that you have not lost sight of it. In doing so, try to give an overview of your essay. This will help the examiner to see your essay as a whole. Another possible technique is to include a quotation from the text in the last line or couple of lines, especially one that refers to the essay question. For example: 'I do believe that the novel deals with "the end of innocence" and "the darkness of man's heart".'

Example 1: grade C answer

> What does Golding think about leaders and leadership in
> *Lord of the Flies* and how does he show this?

The conflict between Ralph and Jack is very important in the novel because this conflict leads to the violence that takes place. The two boys are different types of leader and Golding wants to tell us that without rules people can become like savages.**1**

This is a C-grade standard answer and would need to sum up the cause of the conflict linked to Golding's message clearly to gain a higher grade.

1 This is a clearly written conclusion. The cause of the conflict is not mentioned here. One simple aspect of the writer's message is mentioned.

Example 2: grade A* answer

> Write about Jack and the way Golding presents him in *Lord of the Flies*.

Having looked at the character of Jack and how he leads, it is clear he is a ruthless, violent dictator.**1** Golding has presented him in such a way that we have no doubt of his evil nature.**2** It is therefore interesting that the final mention of Jack in the novel makes him seem a small, helpless boy.**3**

> 'Who's boss here?'
>
> 'I am,' said Ralph, loudly.
>
> A little boy who wore the remains of an extraordinary black cap on his red hair and who carried the remains of a pair of spectacles at his waist, started forward, then changed his mind and stood still' (p. 224).**4**

This shows that he, compared to adults, is merely 'a little boy' and emphasises how childish his actions have been throughout the novel.**5** He is not the leader at the very end as Ralph takes responsibility of leadership when asked by the Officer.**6**

Perhaps this is because he sees himself as still connected to the outside world and he was voted leader, unlike Jack who tells everyone he is now the chief and loses sight of civilised behaviour. Golding has ensured that the evil Jack does not win at the end, but that Ralph survives and therefore there is hope for mankind in that evil does not completely prevail here.**7**

1 Begins summative comments, pointing out Jack as a ruthless and violent character.

2 Mentions Golding's aims of showing Jack's evil nature.

3 Develops point further referring to how he appears at the end of the novel.

4 Supportive quotation included.

5 Explores the quotation and his childish nature, embedding the quotation 'a little boy' into the analysis.

6 Compares Jack to Ralph at the end.

7 Explores Golding's purpose of making Jack this way at the end.

Using quotations and referring to the text

It is essential to use quotations and references to the text in your exam essay. This is to provide evidence for your argument. You can express your personal views on the text — in fact the examiner will be delighted to read something original. However, you must always back them up with this kind of evidence.

Using quotations

One of the most important elements of writing an English literature essay is knowing how to use quotations to support your comments. You will have the text in front of you in the examination, so knowing the words themselves is not an issue. Where candidates fall down is in selecting inappropriate quotations or using too much of the original text. The key to success in this is to be selective.

There are five basic principles to remember when using quotations:

1 Put inverted commas at the beginning and end of the quotation.
2 Write the quotation exactly as it appears in the original.
3 Do not use a quotation that repeats what you have just written.
4 Use the quotation so that it fits into your sentence.
5 Keep the quotation as short as possible.

Quotations should be used to develop the line of thought in your essay. Your comment should not duplicate what is in your quotation. For example do not write:

The author tells us that the naval officer is embarrassed by the boys' tears: 'The officer, surrounded by these noises, was moved and a little embarrassed.'

It would be far more effective to write:

The boys' tears have a profound effect on the naval officer: 'The officer, surrounded by these noises, was moved and a little embarrassed.'

However, the most sophisticated way of using the writer's words is to embed them into your sentence:

The officer is surprised and dismayed that 'a pack of British boys' is not able to 'put up a better show'.

When you use quotations in this way, you are demonstrating that you are able to use text as evidence to support your ideas. You are not simply including words from the original to prove you have read it.

This is particularly important in the exam because of time limitations. Writing out lengthy quotations is time-consuming and proves nothing except your ability to copy, if you have the novel in the exam with you.

You should practise choosing quotations and you could keep a quotations book in which you write down useful words and phrases. This will get you used to thinking about choosing the references to support your comments.

On a technical point, for dialogue (speech), always lay out the lines as they appear in the text. For example:

'Who's boss here?'

'I am,' said Ralph loudly.

Sample essays using quotations

The following question is the sort of question you may get on the OCR specification, but you could be set a question on the fire whichever exam board you are using.

> How does Golding make the fire so important in the novel?
> Support your answer with evidence from the text.

Remember that you are being assessed on AO1 and AO2 in this specification.

When you include quotations in your answer, no matter which board you are using, you need to ensure that you use the PEE format discussed on p. 66. For example:

The fire is significant to the boys and, in particular, to Ralph,**1** because he sees it as the means to ensure they are rescued.**2**

'The fire is the most important thing on the island. How can we ever be rescued except by luck, if we don't keep a fire going?' p. 86 (Chapter 5).**3**

He is frustrated here that the other boys, particularly Jack, are less concerned about the fire and just want to have fun, or hunt for pigs.**4** Golding is showing that the natural instinct of the boys is to have fun and that they are not old enough to behave in a mature/responsible manner.**5**

1 The main point is made about the fire being significant to Ralph.
2 The point is partially explained as it will help them be rescued.
3 A relevant quotation is used to back up the idea.
4 This is explained in a little detail.
5 The best candidates will then go on to find other explanations and to explore ideas further.

Referring to the text

It is not always necessary to use a quotation. If you cannot recall accurately the quotation you want or cannot find it, it is often just as good to refer to it, like this: 'When Ralph is faced with the whole of Jack's tribe, but still tries to persuade everyone that he should be leader, he sounds like a sorry character.'

This technique is also useful if you need to sum up a lengthy passage:

Jack perfects the art of hunting but becomes more savage in the process.

Embedded quotations

You can use brief one or two word quotations in the body of your answer to help illustrate the points you are trying to make as you write. This is a more sophisticated approach to using quotations and can be very effective.

For example:

Note how the candidate embeds quotations from the text into the answer: 'Ralph's lot' and 'tribe' are taken directly from the novel and should be put in quotation marks. This is an effective way of using the text in your answers and helps back up the comments you make in an efficient and impressive manner.

Finally, Jack leaves 'Ralph's lot' and is soon leader of his own 'tribe'.

Some further sections of sample essays are given below. In each case examiners' comments on the answers are provided in blue below the answer. Look at the grade C responses first. You can then set about improving these sections yourself. Once you have done this look at the A* grade responses and compare the kinds of approach in these with the ones that you used.

There is no one correct way to approach an answer but the higher-level responses should give you ideas about how to construct your own.

Character-based questions

Question 1 (foundation tier): AQA-style question

What is Jack like as a leader?
Write about:
- his ideas and actions as a leader and what you think of them
- the techniques Golding uses to show Jack's leadership qualities

This is a typical foundation-tier question: there are bullet points to help you to structure your answer.

Grade C essay

The opening to your essay is very important. It sets the tone for the whole piece of writing. A grade C candidate might write:

Jack is a strong leader in the novel.

Such an opening reflects the demands of the question and makes it clear that you are going to focus on what sort of a leader Jack is. It also avoids falling into the trap of writing a list. (Weaker candidates would probably put the word 'because' after the words 'strong leader in the novel' and end up writing a list.)

The logical thing to do next is to tackle the two bullet points in order — after all, that is why they are there.

His ideas and actions show how strong a leader he is. Jack leads in a dictatorial manner in Lord of the Flies**1** and is violent, aggressive and very effective at getting the other boys to do everything exactly as he wants them to do.**2** His leadership methods are harsh 'The hangman's horror clung over him'**3** and Golding presents Jack in a way that makes us dislike him, making us think that his leadership style is not good.**4**

The style of this answer is very much grade C. There are accurate comments and the answer does not simply retell the story. The reason the

1 Accurate point about character but needs a quotation for support.
2 Sees what Jack is like as a leader and will need to develop these ideas later on.
3 Relevant quotation but does not comment on it.
4 A good point on the writer at work, but needs to develop this with a quotation and exploration of the devices used.

candidate stops moving up the mark scheme beyond grade C is that the answer often says things in the simplest way. The points are correct, but in each case more could be said that would show a deeper understanding of Jack as a leader.

The mark scheme for this question would ask the examiner to look out for:

- sustained response to the presentation of Jack as a leader (AO1)
- effective use of details to support interpretation (AO1)
- explanation of effects of writer's uses of language, structure and form (AO2)
- appropriate comment on themes/ideas and settings (AO2)

These elements are beginning to show here, but are not yet sustained and there is not enough use of details and examination of language used to gain a higher mark.

Grade A* essay

Now look at how an A*-grade candidate might approach a question such as this. In a higher-tier question there would probably be no bullet points to guide you, so let us assume that the question reads:

> Jack and Ralph are two very different leaders. What do you think about their leadership styles and how does Golding present this in *Lord of the Flies*?

An A* candidate knows the importance of opening the answer strongly:

The conflicting leadership styles of Ralph and Jack are central to the plot of Lord of the Flies. It is this conflicting style of leadership that Golding uses to explore the many aspects of human nature that feature in the novel.

This is a strong opening. There is a clear, bold statement that lets the examiner know exactly what the candidate's approach to the answer is. It is obvious from this opening that the candidate recognises the importance of the leadership conflict between the two characters, and the examiner would expect the candidate to develop this idea in the main body of the essay and to give detailed references.

The grade A* answer would tend to give more detailed and more developed comment. The answer might continue like this:

Conflict between Ralph and Jack arises as soon as the two boys meet. Ralph has the initial advantage, as he has already established himself as a person of importance to the younger boys: 'More and more of them came. ... they sat down on the fallen palm trunks and waited.'**1** The boys come to him because Ralph blows

1 Sees the status of Ralph in the eyes of most of the other boys; well-chosen quotation is embedded in the sentence.

2 Sees the link between the old life and the new, and how important a sense of order is to the younger ones.

3 Writes in a detached manner ('the reader'). Good use of embedded quotation again; reads between the lines to see Jack's thoughts.

the conch. They arrive and sit patiently as though they are in a school assembly, showing Ralph's leadership qualities immediately.**2**

Jack arrives at the head of the choir. The way he controls them, 'When his party was about ten yards from the platform he shouted an order and they halted', shows that Jack is already the leader of one section of the boys. The reader immediately suspects that this will lead to trouble between Ralph and Jack, and when Jack's first words are the confrontational 'Where's the man with the trumpet?' it is clear that he does not recognise Ralph as the natural leader of the whole group.**3**

The language used in the higher-tier grade A* answer is more sophisticated than that in the grade C version. The candidate also realises that picking out points that are merely hinted at by the writer — for example that Jack is annoyed at the idea that Ralph is automatically in command — is better than simply recounting an event that is obvious.

Finishing your answer off well is as important as writing a good opening. You should write a short conclusion that sums up the main points of your essay. Do not repeat points word for word. The skilful candidate will keep some comments back until the conclusion, even though they could have been used in the main body of the essay.

The conflict between the two would-be leaders is the central plot device of the novel. It is the catalyst for the violence that takes place and for the resulting breakdown in social order. Golding uses the conflict to show that in the right circumstances even normal people can become violent, savage monsters. The novel serves as a warning to us all about the excesses of human behaviour.

This is a well-written and observant conclusion. It contains clear statements that go beyond simply summing up events. There is a real sense of the deeper message of the novel and a clear final statement about the purpose of the novel as a warning to society.

Overall, this answer has fulfilled the qualities required for an A* response in that it has shown:

- AO1
    - Insightful exploratory response to task, e.g. insightful exploration of what Golding has to say about the conflict in leadership styles between Ralph and Jack.
    - Insightful exploratory response to text, e.g. insightful exploration of Golding's purposes.
    - Close analysis of detail to support interpretation, e.g. unpicking details of Ralph and Jack's thought processes as leaders.
- AO2
    - Evaluation of the writer's uses of language and/or structure and/

or form and effects on readers, e.g. evaluation of use of symbols to show different types of leadership

- Convincing/imaginative interpretation of ideas/themes/settings, e.g. of setting of island as microcosm, reflecting struggle for leadership going on in outside world — this is not mentioned here, but could be in the idol section of the essay and is only one example of the sort of thing that you could include.

All these elements would need to be developed further for the A* to be achieved, but this shows you the skills you are required to show.

Theme-based questions

Not all the questions on the foundation tier will have bullet points to guide you. For example:

What do you think is the importance of the conch in *Lord of the Flies*?

Grade C essay

Symbolically the conch is an important device that Golding uses throughout the novel to show the decline of the boys' behaviour from order to savagery.

The opening again reflects the demands of the question and makes it clear that you are going to focus on the conch and what makes it important in the novel. Again, there is no list of when it is used or what it is used for, which is a good approach.

The first time the conch is described it appears to be very pretty:**1** 'in colour the shell was deep cream, touched here and there with fading pink…delicate embossed pattern' p. 11 (Chapter 1)**2** and Ralph uses it to call the other boys. They all come to him, which shows the power of the conch.**3** It is also the fact that Ralph holds the conch that is a deciding factor when they vote for chief.**4**

1 Accurate point about the conch.
2 Uses a relevant quotation without a comment.
3 Shows the power of the conch.
4 Another purpose of the conch is listed without a quotation for support.

The style of this answer is very much grade C. There are accurate comments and the answer does not simply retell the story. The reason the candidate stops moving up the mark scheme beyond grade C is that the answer often says things in the simplest way. The points are correct, but in each case more could be said that would show a deeper understanding of the purpose of the conch in the novel.

The mark scheme for this question would ask the examiner to look out for:

- sustained response to the presentation of the conch (AO1)
- effective use of details to support interpretation (AO1)

- explanation of effects of writer's uses of language, structure and form (AO2)
- appropriate comment on themes/ideas and settings (AO2)

These elements are beginning to show here, but this is not sustained yet and there is not enough use of details and examination of language used to gain a higher mark.

AO4 (context)

For WJEC to gain a C grade, the mark scheme says:

Candidates:
- are able to set texts in contexts more securely
- begin to see how texts have been influential
- have a clear grasp of social/cultural and historical context
- begin to be able to relate texts to own and others' experience

So, for a question like the one above, you would have to write something about context in your answer. For example:

The conch is like we might use a microphone today.**1** Whoever is holding it is allowed to speak and the others will listen to them, so it represents the boys' disciplined nature. 'I'll give the conch to the next person to speak' p. 31 (Chapter 2).**2**

For most of the novel the boys respect this, but there are notable exceptions.**3** The boys had been brought up at a time when discipline was still harsh in school and the habits they had picked up, like putting their hands up in assembly, were difficult to get rid of.**4** If a group of boys from the 21st century were to be stranded on a desert island, this might be very different, as we do not have the same types of discipline.**5**

Overall, this answer could be said to have elements of three of the bullet points in the WJEC mark scheme, so is well on the way to achieving a C grade, but would need to expand on many of the ideas for a higher mark.

Grade A* essay

How does Golding express ideas about human nature in *Lord of the Flies*?

To achieve an A* grade when answering thematic questions you need the ability to evaluate the whole novel, as well as to look at certain elements in close detail.

To do this successfully it is important to plan carefully what you will write about first (see the section on planning on p. 62).

The mark scheme for the question above may look something like this:
- AO1
  - Insightful exploratory response to task, e.g. insightful exploration

1 The conch is linked with a microphone, so a contextual link has been made.

2 The link is explained and backed up with a relevant quotation, which is not explained.

3 The idea of notable exceptions needs to be explained.

4 A clearer contextual comment is made comparing the boys' schooling to schooling today, with direct comments on discipline. This could be more fully explained.

5 It is suggested that boys today would be different, if stranded on a desert island, but does not go on to suggest how or why, in any detail.

of what Golding has to say about human nature

- – Insightful exploratory response to text, e.g. insightful exploration of Golding's purposes
- – Close analysis of textual detail to support interpretation, e.g. unpicking details about human nature in the novel, such as the descent from order into savagery
- AO2
  - – Evaluation of the writer's uses of language and/or structure and/ or form and effects on readers, e.g. evaluation of use of language and symbols to show human nature
  - – Convincing/imaginative interpretation of ideas/themes/settings, e.g. the destructive nature of the boys, the use of symbols such as the conch, the glasses, the beast all reflecting on a microcosmic nature of this island

All these elements would need to be developed further for the A* to be achieved, but this shows you the skills you are required to show. These paragraphs show you how an argument may develop during an answer.

There is a gradual descent into savagery throughout the novel.**1** From the initial civilised discussions and meetings the boys gradually become more savage and brutal.**2** Golding, by showing this, is exploring the idea that deep inside us we have a darker side that, if left unfettered in the young, could lead to a savage society.**3** Without rules that are reasonable and rational, we can soon degenerate into a savage, animal-like race. He represents this in a number of ways, one of which is by using the conch as a symbol of order.**4** 'We ought to have more rules. Where the conch is, that's a meeting' p. 42:**5** the conch is a symbol of order and organisation, it is shown great respect by the boys, much as we might show respect to someone with a microphone today, as they may have something important to say and it is our human nature to look for symbols of power such as a crucifix, the picture of a powerful leader or a monarch which we can look upon as a mark of respect for that leader.**6** This shows that the majority of humans want to be led by someone powerful, but appealing.

The appeal of Ralph when he is selected as leader is not just his good looks, but the fact that he holds the conch:**7**

> 'there was a stillness about Ralph as he sat that marked him out: there was his size, and attractive appearance; and most obscurely, yet most powerfully, there was the conch.' pp. 18–19**8**

Golding shows us our nature, when selecting a leader, to look for someone who is attractive,**9** which can be seen in many cases with leaders around the world – but not all: Barack Obama is an attractive American leader, but Hitler was far from attractive, but it is vital to note that Hitler was a dictator, Obama was democratically

1 Opening point of this section made clearly.
2 Illustrates point with general textual reference.
3 Begins to explore Golding's purpose.
4 Explores idea with a more detailed, relevant point.
5 Appropriate quotation used to illustrate idea.

6 Analytical exploration of contextual links between symbols used in the text and today.
7 Links Ralph's leadership to good looks and the conch.

8 Relevant quotation employed here.

9 Clear point on how Golding shows our human nature (clear focus on the task).

10 Modern links/
contextualisation is
explored and analysed
further.

11 Convincingly explores
the idea and analyses
it. This is original and
thought-provoking.

12 Concludes point clearly.

elected.**10** Golding is saying that we need some sort of symbol to hold on to as a sign of security, which may explain why today election campaigns normally have posters and pictures as a way of making the public remember a person more.**11** In the absence of such things, the boys fall back on the conch as a symbol of security and reassurance that Ralph is powerful and in control.**12**

Pause for thought

On the WJEC specification AO4 is assessed for context and for an A* grade you are expected to:

- show a clear understanding of social/cultural and historical contexts
- be able to relate texts to own and others' experience
- be able to identify and comment on importance of social/cultural and historical contexts
- show awareness of literary tradition
- be able to relate details of text to literary background and explain how texts have been/are influential at different times

Can you find examples of these points in the answer above? What else does the candidate need to write to gain an A*?

Review your learning

(Answers are given on p. 94.)

1. What is the best way to use a quotation?
2. What might a typical prose text essay contain?
3. What should you say in your essay about the purpose of a text?
4. What are the key features of a good literature essay?
5. How easy is it to move up through the grades?
6. What is the difference between a C grade answer and one that gains an A*?

More interactive questions and answers online.

Answers

Answers to 'Review your learning' questions.

Context (p. 13)

1 The context of a novel is the social, historical and literary factors likely to have influenced the author in writing it.
2 Golding is suggesting that humankind is capable of destroying paradise through aggression, greed and lust for power. There is no real sign of hope from the society that develops on the island. It manages almost to destroy itself, although a higher power does save the boys at the end.
3 Reading the novel today, it is difficult to understand the depth of fear that existed. The possibility of total world war was very real and people were concerned about the kind of world that would be left after such a conflict.
4 The boys begin by obeying the rules of their school and of the society they have left behind. The British idea of being better than everyone else is very strong at the start but soon becomes undermined by the primitive forces that develop on the island.

Plot and structure (p. 28)

1 ● Ralph is made leader
  ● The 'beastie' is seen by a young boy
  ● The fire rages out of control
  ● A ship passes by because the fire has gone out
  ● The hunters kill a pig
  ● The dead parachutist lands on the island and is mistaken for the beast
  ● Jack sets up his own tribe
  ● Simon speaks with the Lord of the Flies and is then killed
  ● Piggy is killed and Ralph is hunted
  ● The navy ship rescues the boys
2 Piggy is important at the start: from the conch to the organisation of the other boys, Piggy plays a vital early role. Once the island becomes more and more ruled by force, Piggy becomes less important. He is finally used as a means to show just how savage Jack's group has become.
  Simon discovers the nature of the beast but has made himself stand out in such a way that he becomes a victim. Golding explores the idea of putting the reader ahead of the central characters through the way he

uses Simon. The reader knows there is no beast before Simon discovers the body on the mountain. His death at the point of telling the others about his find is deliberately dramatic.

3 Golding uses Ralph and Jack both as characters and as symbols of kinds of leadership. The fact that the savage, primitive nature of Jack wins out over the gentle democracy of Ralph reflects the writer's feelings about the nature of boys. It also reflects his feelings about the nature of people in general when placed in a situation where the rules have disappeared. Jack and Ralph are shown as having much in common. Yet despite initial signs of mutual respect, they cannot understand each other's point of view — and Jack soon comes openly to despise Ralph.

4 The world that abandoned the boys ends up rescuing them. They were stranded in the first place because of the war and they are rescued by a warship. Note that Golding specifies that the story ends at the same geographical point on the island as the opening.

Characterisation (p. 42)

1 See the 'Characterisation' section for detailed references about each of the major characters and for quotations that help to define them.

2 Ralph is driven by a desire to do the best for the group and he is influenced by how he thinks adults would handle the situation. He acts democratically.

3 Jack is a dictator. He is violent, punishes those who do not do as he says and likes to rule by fear.

4 ● Ralph is strong and ordered but begins to lose confidence in his own ability. He ends up an outcast from the group he tried to create.

● Jack obeys the rules at first (he wears his choir uniform) but soon allows primitive forces to alter his character.

● Piggy is wise and rational to begin with but his silly ideas about inventions and his lack of strength make him become less important.

● Simon is a victim before the novel starts because of his fits. As the story progresses he reaches a deeper level of understanding that separates him even further from the others.

5 a The relationship between Ralph and Jack is central to the novel and this conflict drives all the other plot elements. These two natural leaders fascinate each other and there is always a close bond between them — initially friendship and then hatred?

b Ralph is sometimes happy to take Piggy's advice but can be cruel to him in public. Piggy displays some hero worship for Ralph but sometimes criticises him in private. Piggy very gradually wins Ralph's trust and affection, and is surprised and grateful.

c Jack gives Roger the opportunity to explore his dark side. Roger does not really want to follow Jack but sees him as a chance to obtain power. Jack is clearly distrustful of Roger but recognises that he is an important means of controlling the other boys.

d Simon follows Ralph but develops his own ideas about life on the island. Simon becomes more detached and less able to explain his thoughts. Ralph thinks Simon can be rather odd and doesn't understand him.

e The littluns act as followers and so give power to whoever is leading the group. They need kindness and affection but are shown little of this. At least Ralph tries to provide shelter for them but the younger children themselves do not realise that Ralph is trying to help them.

Themes (p. 50)

1 Several themes are discussed in this section but you may be able to think of others.

2 Golding is exploring human behaviour in a society without rules, which goes far beyond schoolboys. He is also looking at the possible result of humanity's recent actions (i.e. in the early 1950s). See the *Context* section for a detailed view of this.

3 Golding had a personal interest in how boys would really behave on an island, and a wider concern about where society was heading. The major themes are relevant to the way people live their everyday lives.

4 Look at the *Characterisation* section for an exploration of the way in which certain characters are used to develop the themes of the book.

5 Although the novel was published in 1954, it still has a message for today's reader. There are still nuclear weapons in the world, and many more countries have them than in 1954. Golding's belief in the deterioration of human behaviour under pressure still has a message for us. In addition, the way in which the boys eventually destroy the island is significant today when the threat of global warming as a result of human pollution is so serious for us all.

Style (p. 61)

1 Read 'Setting and atmosphere' at the beginning of this section.

2 Until the death of Piggy, bad events usually happen in darkness or the gloom of the storm. The fact that Piggy is killed in broad daylight indicates how far Jack has lost his sense of right and wrong.

3 See pp. 59 and 87 for further detail.

4 See p. 83 for further detail.

Tackling the exam (p. 70)

1 The word essay means 'an attempt' and is usually one person's thoughts on a given subject. You will find yourself attempting to put across your thoughts on a particular area of the novel when you write in the examination.

2 See 'Planning your answer', on p. 62.

3 See the PEE section on p. 66.

Assessment Objectives and skills (p. 77)

1 Respond to texts critically and imaginatively; select and evaluate relevant textual detail to illustrate and support interpretations.

2 Explain how language, structure and form contribute to writers' presentation of ideas, themes and settings.

3 Relate texts to their social, cultural and historical contexts; explain how texts have been influential and significant to self and other readers in different contexts and at different times.

4 If you are not sure, ask your teacher. Remember:
   - AQA assesses AO1 and AO2
   - OCR assesses AO1 and AO2
   - WJEC assesses AO1 and AO4
   - CCEA assesses AO1 and AO2

5 Do *not* retell the story, quote long passages, identify figures of speech or other features, and give unsubstantiated opinions.

6 See material on p. 76.

Sample essays (p. 90)

1 See 'Quotations' section on p. 81.

2 See 'Essay writing' on p. 78.

3 If the question allows it you should always try to say something about the writer's purpose. This shows that you appreciate that the novel is fiction and not real and that you understand that the writer set out to achieve something specific.

4 Key essay features are discussed in detail in the Essay writing part of this section.

5 You can always work at achieving the next grade up. Be realistic: if you are a grade D three months before the exam you are unlikely to come out with a grade A*, but you can focus on the requirements for grade C.

6 See the grade descriptions on p. 76.